T0316583

Cambridge Elements ≡

Elements in Child Development
edited by
Marc H. Bornstein
National Institute of Child Health and Human Development, Bethesda
Institute for Fiscal Studies, London
UNICEF, New York City

DEPRESSION IN CHILDREN'S LIVES

Keith Crnic

Arizona State University

Betty Lin

University at Albany, State University of New York

CAMBRIDGE
UNIVERSITY PRESS

CAMBRIDGE
UNIVERSITY PRESS

University Printing House, Cambridge CB2 8BS, United Kingdom

One Liberty Plaza, 20th Floor, New York, NY 10006, USA

477 Williamstown Road, Port Melbourne, VIC 3207, Australia

314–321, 3rd Floor, Plot 3, Splendor Forum, Jasola District Centre, New Delhi – 110025, India

103 Penang Road, #05–06/07, Visioncrest Commercial, Singapore 238467

Cambridge University Press is part of the University of Cambridge.

It furthers the University's mission by disseminating knowledge in the pursuit of education, learning, and research at the highest international levels of excellence.

www.cambridge.org
Information on this title: www.cambridge.org/9781108814805
DOI: 10.1017/9781108887144

© Keith Crnic and Betty Lin 2021

First published 2021

A catalogue record for this publication is available from the British Library.

ISBN 978-1-108-81480-5 Paperback
ISSN 2632-9948 (online)
ISSN 2632-993X (print)

Depression in Children's Lives

Elements in Child Development

DOI: 10.1017/9781108887144
First published online: August 2021

Keith Crnic
Arizona State University

Betty Lin
University at Albany, State University of New York

Author for correspondence: Keith Crnic, keith.crnic@asu.edu

Abstract: Although childhood depressive disorders are relatively rare, the experience of depression in children's lives is not. Developmental contextual perspectives denote the importance of considering both depressive disorder and the experience of subclinical depressive symptoms in the child and the family to fully understand the implications of depressive experience for children's developmental well-being. This Element draws on basic emotion development and developmental psychopathology perspectives to address the nature of depressive experience in childhood, both symptoms and disorder, focusing on seminal and recent research that details critical issues regarding its phenomenology, epidemiology, continuity, etiology, consequences, and interventions to ameliorate the developmental challenges inherent in the experience. These issues are addressed within the context of the child's own experience and from the perspective of parent depression as a critical context that influences children's developmental well-being. Conclusions include suggestions for new directions in research on children's lives that focus on more systemic processes.

Keywords: depression, parenting, risk, childhood, internalizing

ISBNs: 9781108814805 (PB), 9781108887144 (OC)
ISSNs: 2632-9948 (online), 2632-993X (print)

Contents

1 Introduction

Children lead rich emotional lives from infancy to puberty and across the multiple contexts in which they engage the meaningful social relationships that define their everyday experiences. In many ways, these emotions dictate the quality of experiences that children have as they negotiate the developmental opportunities and challenges that characterize daily life. Whether positive or negative, emotions serve the adaptive function of supporting development and maintaining well-being (Cole, 2016), and when effectively accomplished across core elements of expressiveness, understanding, and regulation such functions facilitate the development of emotional competence (Denham et al., 2015). In contrast, when emotions are not well managed and become dysfunctional, emotion competence is compromised and problematic affective states, such as depression, may emerge.

A focus on depression in children's lives reflects the fact that depression can be manifest in children's own affective experience, the presence of depressive symptoms or syndrome in parents or close family members, or even its presence in close peers. These multiple affective manifestations are not mutually exclusive, as they can and often do occur in simultaneous contexts. Functional emotion theory (Barrett & Campos, 1987) emphasizes that emotion is inherently relational. The interpersonal context of emotion is especially salient when considering the perspective of depression *in children's lives*, as such a notion embraces the idea that the importance of depressive experience needs to be considered more broadly than as an emotional state that exists within an individual child. Depression in immediate family members exposes children to risk of distress and developmental challenge even though the depression lies other than within the child. Given that emotion is socialized through various processes involving modeling and parental reaction to child emotions (Denham et al., 2015), depression in others, especially parents, provides a critical interpersonal context for the development of intrapersonal distress and subsequent adjustment challenges (Goodman, 2020). Thus, our foci in this Element include depression within the child occurring within the childhood period (0–12 years) and a discussion of the familial context, the impact of parental depression, and other interpersonal relationships that influence children's emerging emotional competence vis-à-vis depressive states.

Emotion and affective processes are at the core of a child's depressive experience, whether that experience is intrapersonal or interpersonal in nature. Emotion is a function of many factors, including individual child temperamental characteristics, genetics, neurobiological considerations, and interpersonal relationships that all transact over time to create specific individual styles and states. Emotional competence "entails successfully navigating a complex inter-personal and intrapersonal world in a flexible, socioculturally appropriate, and effective manner" (Cole, 2016, p. 266). The developmental importance of emotion socialization, especially for young children, cannot be overstated, as parents, teachers, and peers all combine to both intentionally and unintention-ally influence emotion learning and competence (Denham et al., 2015; Eisenberg et al., 1998). As such, when emotion experience becomes comprom-ised or dysregulated, that experience must be considered from contextual as well as intrapersonal perspectives.

Drawing on research and modeling that is international in scope, this Element attempts to provide perspectives on key issues that underlie current conceptualizations relevant to depression in children's lives. The literature on child and parent depression is vast, and an exhaustive review is outside the mission of this Element. Instead, we highlight especially salient concep-tual and empirical work that addresses core issues in each domain. We begin with a discussion of the conceptual bases for a developmental perspective on depression in children's lives and then consider the epidemiological factors that are involved in both child and parental depression. Developmental processes of continuity and discontinuity are considered specific to the childhood period, but with implications for mental health into adolescence and beyond. We review determinants of childhood depres-sion across the spectrum of risk and follow that with a discussion of the consequences of child depressive experience across contexts of depression in the child or in the parenting context. We briefly touch on depression-relevant interventions for children and parents and conclude with perspec-tives on the current state and future needs in regard to depression in children's lives.

2 Current Perspectives on Childhood Depression

Scholarly discussion of depression in childhood has an interesting theoretical history. For some time, children were considered too developmentally and psychologically unsophisticated to experience depression, or the possibility of depressive experience in children was thought to be masked by the expression of other disorders (Rao & Chen, 2009). Such views gave way to research in the mid to later part of the twentieth century that indicated that depression was not solely an adult disorder. Furthermore, the emergence of developmental psycho-pathology as a framework for conceptualizing childhood disorder provided the impetus for understanding that depression in childhood could be conceived in its own right and not simply as a downward extension of adult depression

(Cicchetti et al., 1994). Indeed, the manifestation of depression was thought to vary as a function of developmental stage (Cicchetti & Toth, 1998).

In constructing their developmental psychopathology perspective on childhood depression, Cicchetti and Toth (1998) proposed an organizational model of depressotypic development that gives prominent consideration to physiological and affective regulation processes, attachment, and self-system development as key to understanding the emergence of depressive experience in children within the context of ongoing transactional ecological influences. Developmental perspectives help to illuminate the emergence of depressive symptoms and experience through models and mechanisms built to understand the ways in which existing child risk factors transact with ongoing contextual and interpersonal processes to affect children's emotional distress. Emotional dysfunction then is reflected in situations in which emotion processes compromise developmental competence and is a central component of multiple disorders of childhood, including mood disorders (Cole, 2016). Indeed, deficits in emotional competence typically precede some forms of psychopathology, including depression, and tend to support maintenance and intensification of symptoms (Cole, 2016).

Negative emotionality comprises a number of individual states, including fear, anger, sadness, and irritability. Sadness is a core emotional state associated with diagnosis of depression in children, but it is also a basic emotional state common to childhood. Sadness may function to lead to withdrawal after loss, serving some adaptive purpose in conserving resources (Clifford et al., 2015), but it also serves to promote cognitive restructuring necessary to promote adaptation when individual goals may be thwarted in some important way (Karnaze & Levine, 2018). So, although sadness is one of the negative emotions that predicts internalizing problems, it remains important to differentiate normative sad affective experience from the dysregulated processes that may lead to depressive symptoms or disorder. Furthermore, depression as currently conceptualized reflects a constellation of emotional and behavioral symptoms that extend well beyond sadness as a defining attribute.

2.1 Symptoms, Syndrome, Disorder

Current conceptualizations of depression suggest that depressive experience can be differentiated along three dimensions that describe levels at which the phenomenon can operate. Those three levels involve the notions of *symptoms*, *syndrome*, and *disorder*, which represent a hierarchical ordering of the extent to which the construct of depression can be largely described and experienced, and by which most research on depressive processes has been focused. We address each of these dimensions in what follows.

2.1.1 Symptoms

Symptoms reflect the individual indicators of children's (or adults') depressive experience. They include the affective, cognitive, behavioral, and physiological components that represent basic attributes of depression. The hallmark symptoms for children are sad mood and irritability (Bufferd et al., 2017; Hankin, 2017) but also include a wealth of other indicators that can vary as a function of age and context. Individual symptoms can be discerned from diagnostic classification indicators, such as the *Diagnostic and Statistical Manual of Mental Disorders* (5th ed.; DSM-5; American Psychiatric Association, 2013), or from studies that explore attributes that are found in children who are at risk or in some way identified as showing signs of depression. Weiss and Garber (2003) identified a set of twenty-nine individual symptoms that include other frequently studied indicators across markers of affect, behavior, and physiological or vegetative concern (Table 1), delineating the heterogeneity in symptoms that are associated with depressive conditions in childhood. At the symptom level of analysis, no assumption is made about the presence or absence of other symptoms or indicators of depression (Compas et al., 1993). The symptom level offers a description of just how depressed children present on individual indicators, providing information relevant to assessment processes as well as epidemiological concerns.

Among the twenty-nine symptoms identified in the Weiss and Garber (2003) meta-analysis, twenty-three offered some evidence that the symptom varied across ages, although the variability was not consistent across studies included in the analysis. Moderators such as child sex, sampling (diagnostic versus nonclinical groups), and informants (parent, child, interviewer) helped to partially explain differences in the variability observed. Weiss and Garber (2003) cautioned that the basic tests of main effect differences engaged by these symptom-based studies could not account for whether differences in symptoms were simply a function of normative developmental change over time. More extensive discussion of continuity in childhood depression can be found in Section 4.2.

2.1.2 Syndrome

The syndrome level of analysis treats depression as a constellation of behaviors, thoughts, and emotions that tend to co-occur, typically identified through multivariate analytic methods. As Compas and colleagues (1993) noted, there

Table 1 Symptoms associated with childhood depression.

Effect size (ES) heterogeneity and mean by symptom

Symptom	N	Q	Mean ES
1. Agitation	11	16.76****	
2. Anhedonia	15	3.17	0.11****
3. Anorexia	15	12.52**	
4. Appetite problems	5	5.07**	
5. Concentration	13	18.82****	
6. Fatigue	18	28.30****	
7. Guilt	16	14.08*	
8. Hopelessness	14	1.62	0.19***
9. Hyperexia	10	20.99****	
10. Hypersomnia	12	5.03	0.16***
11. Insomnia	14	9.24*	
12. Irritable	14	10.67*	
13. Retardation	15	16.48**	
14. Sadness (nonverbal)	12	17.40***	
15. Sadness (verbal)	13	12.05**	
16. Self-esteem	19	62.67****	
17. Sleep problems	10	1.82	−0.04
18. Suicide	20	40.51****	
19. Weight gain	6	1.48	0.28****
20. Weight loss	6	15.34***	
21. Anxiety	19	81.38****	
22. Delusions	5	23.71****	
23. Externalizing	15	11.99	−0.04
24. Hallucinations	10	1.98	−0.03
25. Increased energy	3	0.18	−0.12**
26. Social withdrawal	16	8.06	0.09***
27. Somatic complaints	13	15.84**	
28. Somatic concerns	7	0.63	0.02
29. Worse in morning	4	34.23****	

Note. Q, Q statistic for testing the heterogeneity of effect sizes (Hedges & Olkin, 1985).
*$p < 0.10$. **$p < 0.05$. ***$p < 0.01$. ****$p < 0.001$. For the probability that the heterogeneity differs significantly from chance expectations or that the mean effect is not equal to zero.
Source. From Weiss and Garber (2003, p. 419)

is no implied nature or cause to the symptoms, and differences between individuals are viewed simply as statistical deviations in the degree to which various symptoms are expressed.

Rarely do studies focus expressly on child or parent sad or dysphoric mood. Rather, most studies explore depression as indexed by a variety of symptoms presented on checklist measures or combinations of checklists, interviews, or observations. Mood is always central, but multiple related cognitive, behavioral, and affective symptoms are also present without concern as to the extent to which symptoms are necessarily persistent or impairing (Hankin, 2017). A multifactor syndrome level of analysis that looks for the relations among symptoms within and across ages offers better explanations of potential etiologies and more complex age differences than does the symptom approach (Weiss & Garber, 2003).

The syndrome level also represents the range or extent of depressive function without necessarily implying whether the level may be clinically meaningful. Some research applying syndrome-level approaches found differences in the structure of the depressive syndrome between child and adolescent groups, with indications that guilt and externalizing symptoms may be more frequent symptoms in childhood whereas anhedonia and sad affect may be more prevalent symptoms in adolescence (Weiss et al., 1992). Other syndrome-level approaches using factor analytic or network structures to identify connections among symptoms in nonclinical samples likewise show differences between child and adolescent symptoms but also suggest that anxiety is difficult to differentiate from depression in children under twelve (Cole et al., 1997; McElroy et. al., 2018). It may be that some combined depression-anxiety factor best represents an internalizing dimension during childhood, and the two dimensions may not begin to clearly differentiate until adolescence.

2.1.3 Disorder

The disorder level of analysis represents a categorical indicator of the presence or absence of a condition in which a set of symptoms (a syndrome) exists with sufficient chronicity and severity as to create notable distress and/or impairment in an individual's ability to appropriately function in their daily lives. Disorder implies the presence of a "clinical diagnosis" and differentiates those who meet the diagnostic conditions for disorder from those who do not.

The criteria for the diagnosis of a major depressive disorder are identified in the DSM-5 (American Psychiatric Association, 2013), the latest version of the predominant classification manual. There is little differentiation in DSM between children and adults in the diagnostic criteria for depressive disorder, with relatively minor exceptions. To meet criteria for diagnosis, children must show depressed or sad mood almost every day for two weeks. For children, irritability can replace sad mood as the predominant descriptive symptom. At least four other symptoms must also be present from a list that includes anhedonia, sleep disturbance, difficulty concentrating, weight gain or loss, hopelessness or helplessness, fatigue, and suicidal ideation.

Beyond major depressive disorder, there are two other disorders relevant to children: persistent depressive disorder (PDD) and disruptive mood dysregulation disorder (DMDD). PDD captures more chronic depressive conditions that extend for at least a year in children and includes the previous dysthymic diagnosis (less severe but persistent feelings of sadness or depressed mood). DMDD is a newer category that was created to obviate the challenges inherent in diagnosing bipolar disorder in children (Copeland et al., 2013). Rather than focusing on lability or changes in mood, DMDD is characterized by chronic irritability lasting more than twelve months with the periodic occurrence of extreme tantrums that are out of proportion to the situation in which they happen (SAMHSA, 2016).

Research at the level of disorder typically includes only those children and/or their parents as participants who have received a diagnosis of depression, typically by a trained diagnostician who can reliably and validly identify the presence of the disorder. The focus of such studies is generally to differentiate disorder from non-disorder with respect to characteristics, risks, and process or mechanisms through which disorder is affected and affects developmental functions.

2.2 Interplay of the Hierarchy

Most research that addresses depression in children's lives focuses on depression at either the symptom or the syndrome level (Hankin, 2017). In effect, these approaches adopt the premise that depression is actually a dimensional construct rather than a categorical one. The DSM approach, which sets specific criteria for disorder, is more categorical and implies that one either meets the necessary criteria for depression or does not. In the dimensional approach, depressive symptoms exist on a continuum from low to high, and depression itself represents the more extreme end of the continuum of affective processes. The conflict between these opposing perspectives has been a focus of both theoretical and empirical interest over the years, in arguments as to whether depressive disorder reflects a level of functioning that can be considered qualitatively different from the affective experience of others who do not meet the stringent diagnostic criteria. In contrast, the dimensional perspective suggests that the difference between disorder and subclinical manifestations is one of degree rather than kind, such that sadness or dysphoric affect is common to human experience and non-disorder reflects levels of dysphoric affect that fall below the threshold that dictates distress and impairment in daily living.

The controversy between dimensional and categorical (taxonic) perspectives has largely been resolved in favor of more dimensional perspectives, at least with respect to depression. In a sophisticated taxometric analysis of adult depression, Rucsio and Rucsio (2000) found that a latent depression taxon (an underlying categorical structure) could not be detected across two large samples, and evidence supported a more dimensional or quantitative model. Subsequently, Hankin and colleagues (2005) found similar support for the dimensional perspective in a large population-based sample of children and adolescents. They showed that, for both children and adolescents, evidence favored a more dimensional approach to identifying a latent structure for depression. Furthermore, neither child age nor sex significantly impacted the level of support for a dimensional perspective. Beauchaine and Hinshaw (2020) have also described how the use of DSM-defined syndromes in research is problematic for uncovering the nature of child psychopathologies due to the heterogeneity inherent in diagnostic criteria, including those for mood disorders. Even with respect to clinical interventions, symptom concerns have been found to drive decisions more so than have diagnoses per se (Waszczuk et al., 2017).

Essentially, the dimensional perspective supports the specific salience of the symptom and syndrome levels of analysis for exploring depressive functioning in children, as well as in adult parents. Symptoms support the emergence of syndromes, and syndromes in turn support the emergence of disorder to the extent that severity and chronicity thresholds are met. The dimensional perspective also aligns well with developmental psychopathology perspectives. The interplay of risk and resilience processes across contexts and in transaction allows for the natural variability observed in depressive symptoms during childhood as well as for the changing multifactor structure of symptoms over time. Disorder perspectives remain relevant and important to defining populations for study, although the varying or multiple ways in which the criteria for diagnosis can be met challenges the utility of categorical approaches for some research purposes.

In sum, the symptom, syndrome, and disorder levels of analysis provide a rich array of approaches for exploring the nature of depressive experience in both children and parents. Although depressive experience seems to conform best to dimensional perspectives, categorical approaches remain both relevant and important in establishing criteria for research on specific diagnostic groups and in multiple clinical applications. Both perspectives are key to identifying the extent and salience of depressive experience in children's lives.

3 Epidemiology of Depression in Children's Lives

Sadness, unhappiness, distress, and irritability are ubiquitous affective experiences in childhood, and so whereas these affective conditions can be considered as "symptoms" in studies that focus on depression, they are also normative emotion states that have few clinical implications. Indeed, most children's experience of these negative affective states fall well within the normal variation of everyday emotion, and clinical depression in childhood is relatively rare before age twelve. Most reports suggest that rates of clinically meaningful depression for children under twelve are 1–2 percent generally and less than 3 percent for lifetime prevalence (Egger & Angold, 2009; Hankin, 2017). Incidence of depression in children has been found to be higher in families experiencing poverty or having a low socioeconomic position (Goodman et al., 2011; Joinson et al., 2017), but not always (LeMoult et al., 2020). Rates of depression in prepubertal boys and girls are fairly similar, in contrast to adolescence and adulthood when rates in females are substantially higher than for males (Egger & Angold, 2009; Garber & Rao, 2014). Overall rates of depression increase into adolescence and adulthood, but younger children seldom meet the criteria for a specific depression diagnosis, and diagnoses are rarer still in infants and preschoolers. However, this does not mean that subclinical levels of depressed mood, sad affect, or irritability do not create levels of risk for children's well-being, depending on the extent to which such "symptoms" are apparent. As discussed in Section 6 of this Element, studies of children's negative affectivity that focus on mood and sadness indicate that higher levels of such affect, albeit subclinical, are associated with more adverse developmental outcomes across childhood (Wesselhoeft et al., 2016).

With respect to possible ethnic differences in depressive symptoms in children, the evidence is mixed. Some research finds support for increased depressive symptoms among Latin American children, in comparison to European American and African American children (Twenge & Nolen-Hoeksema, 2002). Other studies comparing ethnic groups found no differences in the prevalence of depressive disorders between European American and African American children (Angold et al., 2002) or between European American and Native American youth (Costello et al., 1997). Nevertheless, the relatively small sample sizes for ethnic minority children in most studies present challenges to fully identifying the prevalence of depressive disorders across specific groups.

Although depression in children may be relatively rare, depression is quite a bit more prevalent in adult parents and appears to be most prevalent during infancy and early childhood periods. In a cohort study of almost 87,000 mother–father–child triads, Davé and colleagues (2010) reported overall incidences of 7.5 percent and 2.7 percent for mothers and fathers, respectively, but these figures were higher during the first year postpartum. Across the childhood period, they reported that 39 percent of mothers and 21 percent of fathers had experienced at least one episode of depression, identified by primary care diagnostic notation or through prescribed antidepressants. The rates of parental depression are higher than the rates of depression found in the general population of adults (Ramchandani et al., 2005). These are disturbingly high numbers and suggest that children are exposed to parental depression at what might be considered alarmingly high rates. However, Goodman (2010) cautioned that these figures, high as they are, may even underestimate children's exposures. She suggested that there is a variety of reasons for the likely underestimation, including potential reporting or measurement limitations and the fact that many parents may function at subclinical levels of depression that create meaningful risks for children but are not necessarily sufficient to indicate a diagnostic condition or need for medication. Regardless, the extent to which depression reflects a potentially meaningful element in children's lives is not simply dependent on the child's own internal experience but includes those systemic contexts most proximal to their developmental well-being. Indeed, research supports direct connections between parent and child trajectories of depressive symptoms (Garber et al., 2011).

4 Developmental Expression and Continuity

DSM classifications and descriptions have long been criticized for being a-developmental. That is, they do not well address the developmental differences, ontogenetic processes, and changes that are endemic to the childhood period (0–12 years). Depression diagnoses have been a good example of this a-developmental approach given that the diagnostic criteria for children and adults are essentially the same. However, research from the developmental psychopathology perspective has provided a wealth of evidence that there are important developmental differences that need to be considered. Indeed, there is evidence that depressive symptoms vary as a function of the developmental levels of the child, wherein different symptoms may exert their influence at different times, and distinctive constellations of symptoms may characterize depression at differing child ages (Weiss & Garber, 2003). The course of childhood depressive experience, particularly the continuity of depression across the childhood period and its implications for later behavioral and developmental well-being, is of critical concern. Likewise, accounting for the experience of depression in children's lives, the timing, expression, and chronicity of parental depressive experience are also important and are addressed in turn.

4.1 Expression Across Childhood

Although the core symptoms of depression are common to all ages, there are differences in the symptoms that children express both in comparison to adolescent and adult depression and in the nature of symptoms across the childhood period. It should not be surprising to find that symptoms vary as a function of age, as basic orthogenetic principles operate to influence biological, cognitive, linguistic, emotional, and social competencies over time and serve to shape the ways in which children express, understand, and experience depressive states.

With regard to expression and identification of depressive experience in children, the ability to express and verbally describe psychiatric symptoms – including anxiety and depressive symptoms – may be limited by language development and cognitive factors. This concern emerges particularly with younger children. As such, psychiatric assessments commonly rely on parents/caregivers and other reliable informants, such as teachers, to provide information about symptoms or expression, as children are thought to be unreliable reporters of their own mental state (Luby et al., 2007). However, adult reporters may fail to accurately recognize mood symptoms in younger children; therefore, corroborating evidence concerning symptoms from the child's own perspective would be of value in a clinical diagnostic assessment. Indeed, there is some evidence that children as young as preschool age can reliably report on core symptoms, although not on more complex symptoms of the disorders (Luby et al., 2007).

4.1.1 Infancy

As noted in Section 2, there was some debate as to whether infants were developmentally capable of experiencing or expressing depression. However, infant mental health perspectives suggest that early relevant symptoms may be present but clinical disorders themselves may simply not be fully differentiated during infancy (Zeanah & Zeanah, 2009). Infants with depressive features show somewhat different expression than do preschoolers and not surprisingly with school-age children. Depressive symptoms common to infancy include fussiness, feeding and sleeping problems, apathy, withdrawal, attachment concerns, and restricted social play (Fristad & Black, 2018; Guedeney, 2007). Infant depressive symptoms also align well with nonorganic failure to thrive, which has been considered as a manifestation of infant mood disturbance.

Infant depression is also highly aligned with the presence of postpartum depression in caregivers. In fact, it is difficult to find research that focuses exclusively on infant depression as opposed to studies that explore infant affective reaction to parental mood disorder. This is not surprising as infant affective response is primarily coregulated through interaction with a parent or adult caregiver, and research suggests both adverse (Mesman et al., 2009) and resilient (Davis et al., 2019) infant affective response to maternal depression. We address the important context of parental postpartum depression as well as antenatal depression in Section 5.3.

4.1.2 Preschool

Toddler and preschool ages have been suggested to be a sensitive period for the onset of depressotypic organization due to the cognitive, social, and emotional development that marks this period (Cicchetti & Toth, 1998). Luby and colleagues (2003, 2009c) have described and differentiated depression during the preschool years to understand its nature and developmental consequences. Sad affect, lethargy across contexts, irritability, as well as sleep and feeding disturbances are symptoms shared with other age groups to one extent or another, but Luby and colleagues have suggested that anhedonia during play, the action of self-conscious emotions such as shame and inappropriate guilt (Luby et al., 2009b), as well as extreme fatigue are key differentiators of depression in preschoolers and may be pathognomonic markers of depression. Their work also indicated that, at preschool ages, it may be important to modify diagnostic requirements that symptoms be present for a minimum of two weeks. Requiring the temporal criteria resulted in missing a group of preschoolers with clinically significant depression that produced two-year developmental outcomes similar to those preschool-age children who met the two-week criteria (Gaffrey et al., 2011; Luby et. al., 2002).

Although irritability and sadness are normative preschool behaviors as well as core symptoms at this age (Leppert et al., 2019), Luby and colleagues (2009a) found that they are nonspecific markers in relation to other disorders such as anxiety. Despite the developmental significance of its major characteristics, developmental delay is not associated with depression in preschoolers. Research has done much to establish the salience of depressive symptoms at this developmental period for preschooler psychological well-being and its implications for understanding early mental health.

4.1.3 Childhood

In the childhood period (ages 6–12 years), depressive experience becomes more visible as children enter school and face a variety of new challenges in their lives. Children now have the capacity to engage in more complex cognitive actions and can entertain meaningful ideas about their self and future that undergird the ability to experience depressive symptoms. Sad mood is a predominant characteristic, but children also show symptoms of clinging to adults, tearfulness, increased irritability, anhedonia, hopelessness, hypersomnia, and social withdrawal (Fristad & Black, 2018; Weiss & Garber, 2003). These symptoms are more frequent in school-age children than during infancy or the preschool period but still have a relatively low frequency overall. In a study of nearly 1,000 children and adolescents with major depressive disorder, Yorbik and colleagues (2004) added low self-esteem as a symptom in addition to the others already listed here and noted that these symptoms tended to be associated with specific events or specific thoughts as opposed to more generalized distress. Thus, the childhood period is marked by a more sophisticated cognitive presentation of symptoms and greater breadth to the behavioral and social markers of depressive experience.

4.2 Continuity in Childhood Depression

The indications that symptoms vary as a function of child age raise the important need to understand the nature of continuity in depression across the childhood period and whether there are potential ramifications of depression in childhood for the presence of depressive experience in adolescence and adulthood. Certainly, an organizational perspective on development suggests that continuity and discontinuity, whether lawful or not, are critical to understanding the nature of how depression operates in children's lives. Indeed, issues of continuity in childhood depression have been of conceptual significance for many years and are multifaceted and complex in the processes involved. Continuity, which involves consistency of group means over time, can be differentiated from stability, which more reflects individual rank order within groups over time (Bornstein et al., 2017). Although it seems to be the case that children who experience depression do not necessarily become depressed adults, adults who experience depression were likely to have experienced some depressive episode during childhood. This greater likelihood of backward mapping is similar to other disorders of childhood and reflects the importance of multifinality as a prominent mechanism in development generally and in developmental psychopathology in particular (Cicchetti & Toth, 1998).

Although childhood depression may not be clearly deterministic in relation to the experience of depression later in adult life, continuity and discontinuity across the infancy through childhood period are important for children's individual well-being, their functional competencies across academic and social contexts, and the risks for problems in adolescence and beyond. This is true despite the fact that research suggests that depressive symptoms seem to decrease from age six to twelve (Cohen et al., 2018; Kim & Cicchetti, 2006), and actual major depressive disorder is relatively rare prior to puberty (Garber & Rao, 2014). The relative rarity and symptom decrease do not, however, lessen the salience of the concern for the developmental implications of continuity of depressed mood from infancy through the childhood period.

The multifaceted nature of continuity can be seen from the various ways in which it is construed, the ways it is measured, and the factors that appear to influence it (e.g., child sex, comorbidity, socioeconomic status [SES], etc.). Furthermore, studies of continuity in childhood depression do not all converge toward a single understanding of the issue or the factors that operate to influence it. There is likely a myriad of reasons for this in the research literature, including sampling differences, variations in measurement approaches to depression, more or less specialized analytic frameworks to identify relations over time, and variability in the inclusion of meaningful covariates. This is obviously not an exhaustive list but provides some sense of why findings diverge with respect to understanding how depression manifests and persists across the period from infancy to later childhood.

Weiss and Garber (2003) described continuity as involving two processes: that which occurs within the individual and addresses whether the presence of depression recurs over time; and that which reflects the form or the characteristics of the depressive episode and varies at differing developmental stages. Homotypic continuity is exemplified by the situation in which symptoms are the same over time or when following some developmental transition point. Heterotypic continuity, in contrast, reflects the situation in which the specific symptom expression at one point in time leads to a different symptom expression at a later point in time although the underlying higher-order construct is the same.

Some studies suggest that the recurrence of childhood depression is quite high, perhaps as much as 50–70 percent (Maughan et al., 2013). However, even those high rates suggest that around 40 percent of children who experience a depressive episode never experience a recurrence (Hankin, 2017). Individual symptoms during childhood are generally considered to be somewhat more stable than disorder per se (Garber & Rao, 2014; Luby et al., 2014), but the degree to which stability is found appears at least to some extent to depend on the amount of time between assessments and the source of the reports (teachers, parents, interviewers, or children). Early symptom onset (preschool ages) seems to be associated with greater risk of symptom recurrence and the presence of major depressive disorder in later childhood, even when controlling for maternal depression (Luby et al., 2014). Yet still, many children who experience early episodes of depressive symptoms do not sustain significant mood disturbance.

A number of studies have examined growth trajectories of depression or depressive symptoms across the childhood period, attempting to identify variations in continuity for childhood depression. Some commonalities have emerged across studies, as have some unique perspectives. In a sample of more than 2,000 Dutch children assessed between the ages of four and eighteen years, Dekker and colleagues (2007) identified six trajectory groups that differed not only in the levels of depression but also in the timing of onset and the shape of curves produced. One group of girls showed childhood onset of more significant depression that increased over time, whereas boys did not show such a pattern. The hypothesized high-stable trajectory of depression for boys could not be identified in that sample. Similar sex differences in children's depression trajectories were noted by Lewis and colleagues (2020). However, Tram and Cole (2006) found that child sex did not differentiate the stability of depressive symptoms in a two-cohort study of more than 1,200 school-age children from the United States.

Comorbidity is common in childhood symptoms, especially among internalizing symptoms. Even disruptive behavior disorders have shown clear comorbidities with childhood depression. Comorbidity can complicate understandings of depressive experience in childhood, as these related emotion and behavioral concerns can impact the expression and course of depressive experience. Studies of symptom trajectories have addressed the comorbidities associated with depression with respect to the way that such comorbidities affect the continuity of depressive functioning for children. In exploring comorbidities between anxiety and depression during childhood, Cohen and colleagues (2018) hypothesized two distinct pathways for the expression of depressive symptoms across childhood and into adolescence. One involved a discontinuous homotypic pattern in which the absence of depressive symptoms in childhood precedes the emergence of depressive symptoms in adolescence, and the other involved a discontinuous heterotypic pattern in which early anxiety symptoms in childhood might predict depressive symptoms in adolescence. Using piecewise growth curve modeling, Cohen and colleagues (2018) found that childhood anxiety did not forecast depression in adolescence, but childhood depression did forecast adolescent depression and anxiety, providing evidence in support of both homo- and heterotypic continuity. Furthermore, their data supported age twelve as a developmental knot, the point at which symptoms change course and trajectories become discontinuous. In a study of comorbidity between conduct problems and depression, McDonough-Caplan and colleagues (2018) reported no differences in depression growth for children with either depression or conduct problems, and whereas depression symptoms in childhood were not associated with conduct problems in adolescents, conduct problems in childhood did forecast depression in adolescence. It seems apparent that the comorbidity that is typical of childhood psychopathology, whether clinical or subclinical in nature, has important implications for the continuity of childhood depression.

In summary, continuity of childhood depression appears to involve a complex process for which we do not yet have all the answers to understand the way it works. Although there is some evidence of risk for recurrent episodes across childhood, sizeable numbers of children do not show recurrences. Continuity modifiers, such as child sex, comorbidities, SES, and age at onset play important roles in determining the degree of individual continuity. Given that depressive symptoms appear to show greater continuity during childhood than does disorder, however, it may be that depressive experience slips above and below clinically meaningful levels over time and remains a risk for emotional and behavioral well-being.

4.3 Continuity in Parental Depression

The extent to which children experience recurrent or ongoing depressive mood has important implications for their well-being across a variety of functional domains, but the continuity of exposure to parental depression likewise carries clear developmental risk. Parental depression, from antenatal to postpartum to occurrence at any point across the childhood period is not uncommon, as the evidence from Davé and colleagues (2010) indicates. Consequently, many children must cope with parental depressive states and the minor and major adversities that these states bring. Also, extensive review of the relations between maternal depression and children's psychological functioning suggests that children have clear risk for more problematic outcomes when mothers are depressed, but several key modifiers operate to dictate the nature of those risks (Bornstein et al., in press; Goodman et al., 2011). Evidence has also accrued to show similar adverse effects related to paternal depression during childhood (Cheung & Thiele, 2019), and research indicates that adverse effects of depression on parenting behavior are similar for mothers and fathers (Wilson & Durbin, 2010).

Given the potential influence of parental depression on children's general behavioral and emotional competence, and for the emergence of childhood depression in particular, it is important to understand whether differences in timing and chronicity of parental depression may have differing implications for children's experience. Across the childhood period, the evidence seems to suggest that parents are reasonably susceptible to experiencing a depressive episode, as close to 40 percent report depression at least one time prior to their child's age twelve (Ahun et al., 2017; O'Connor et al., 2017; Turney, 2012). In a sample of more than 1,300 women, Campbell and colleagues (2009) assessed maternal depressive symptoms from child age one to twelve years and identified five latent classes of parents: never depressed, stable subclinical, early decreasing, moderately elevated, and chronically depressed mothers. The percentage of mothers within each class was 49 percent, 4 percent, 30 percent, 11 percent, and 5 percent, respectively, again suggesting that 40 percent or more of mothers report depressive symptoms above normative levels. Highly persistent or chronic depression was rarer across all the studies, typically below 10 percent. Similarly, Putnick and colleagues (2020) identified four trajectory groups of nearly 5,000 depressed mothers postpartum and found that, although 25 percent of mothers reported at least moderate depressive symptoms in the three years postpartum, only 4.5 percent showed persistently high depressive symptoms. There is not nearly the data available to understand the chronicity and severity of paternal depression, as most of the study of depression in fathers is focused on the antenatal and postpartum periods. Nevertheless, rates of depression during these periods have been found to be as high as 10 percent for men (Ballard & Davies, 1996), and, in general, men are considered to have about half the rate of depression as women during the ages most associated with childrearing (Wilson & Durbin, 2010). Nevertheless, the extent to which we understand the chronicity and continuity of depression in fathers remains limited.

The research on chronicity of depression in parents suggests that children are broadly exposed to depressive symptoms in parents at a fairly frequent rate. This exposure ranges from relatively mild symptoms to full major depressive disorder, and the exposure can begin as early as the prenatal period. The evidence suggests that depressive states may be highest or most frequent during the postpartum period and may be less apparent during school age, but persistent depression expressed as symptoms, syndrome, or disorder is a common exposure for children worldwide (Arifin et al., 2018).

5 Risk Factors and the Emergence of Childhood Depression

Research investigating vulnerability factors for the onset of childhood depression indicates that, although no single causal factor can predict the onset of childhood depression, several child, family, and contextual risk factors can increase the probability that children will develop a depressive disorder. Importantly, many of these factors are interrelated and likely heighten vulnerability in transaction with one another. Nevertheless, we discuss them as discrete constructs here for the sake of accessibility and try to point out some of the ways in which they may intersect.

5.1 Child Factors

Several risk factors for depressive experience involve child-specific characteristics and processes. Among those considered here are genetic, biological, temperamental, social-cognitive, and a range of family, peer, and contextual factors that operate to influence the development of depressive experience during childhood.

5.1.1 Genetic Processes

A family history of depression has repeatedly emerged as one of the most robust predictors of childhood depression (Beardselee et al., 1998). Children with first-degree relatives (e.g., parents, siblings) with depression experience approximately three times more risk for developing childhood depression compared to those without (Rice et al., 2002; Williamson et al., 2004). Although at first blush this seems to imply the relative importance of genetics in the ontogeny of childhood depression, studies considering family histories of depression cannot actually discern whether associations reflect genetic or environmental effects. In fact, heritability studies utilizing twin and adoption designs have yielded limited support for the genetic bases of childhood depression (Rice et al., 2002). Instead, environmental influences (e.g., early life stressors, interpersonal relationships) appear to represent the primary contributors to childhood depression (Gjerde et al., 2019; Rice et al., 2002).

The role of environmental influences in the emergence of childhood depression is further exemplified when considering how associations between genetics and depression change across development. Specifically, in contrast to heritability studies of depression in childhood, heritability studies of depression in adolescence have yielded findings suggestive of moderate levels of heritability (Rice et al., 2002). This increased heritability may reflect the increased salience of gene–environment correlations as children begin to exert more control over their environments (Rice, 2010; Thapar & Rice, 2006). That is, rather than an increase in genetic contributions across childhood, children's greater capacities to actively select and shape their environments over time in ways that amplify risk for depression are believed to underlie this change.

In summary, genetics appear to contribute minimally to risk for depression before age eleven years. Instead, environmental factors appear to play a more prominent role during this time. Nevertheless, work considering changes in the heritability of depression over time underscores the salience of gene–environment transactions for amplifying risk processes and suggests that genetically based child characteristics are also of great relevance for understanding the development of childhood depression.

5.1.2 Biological Factors

Among the vast array of biological susceptibility factors that have been studied (Garber & Rao, 2014; Kaufman et al., 2001), abnormalities with biological stress responsivity and neural connectivity have emerged as prominent biological substrates underlying childhood depression.

5.1.2.1 Biological Stress Responsivity

Given the prominent role that environmental stressors play in the ontogeny of childhood depression, it is not surprising that the biological systems that modulate the stress response have also been implicated to play a role in the onset of childhood depression. As has been reviewed in detail elsewhere (Ulrich-Lai & Herman, 2009), the stress response system comprises three major subsystems. The *parasympathetic nervous system (PNS)*, or the "rest and digest" system, generally functions to reduce arousal and promote rest. The *sympathetic nervous system (SNS)*, or the "fight or flight" system, functions to increase arousal and readiness to respond to threats. The *hypothalamic–pituitary–adrenocortical (HPA) axis*, initiates the longer-term response to stress and functions to increase arousal and vigilance as well as to modulate the defensive activities triggered by the SNS to promote recovery. Together, these three systems function hierarchically in response to stress, with the PNS acting first (i.e., by disengaging or withdrawing), followed by the SNS, and finally the HPA axis (Porges, 2007). Most research exploring stress response abnormalities tied to childhood depression has focused on the contributions of the HPA axis and the PNS.

The HPA axis has been a subject of prime interest in studies of childhood depression given a half-century of research suggesting that HPA hyperactivity represents a robust biomarker of depression among adults (Stetler & Miller, 2011). In fact, this finding has emerged with such consistency that it has even been declared "one of the most consistent biological findings in major depression psychiatry" (Pariante & Lightman, 2008, p. 464). HPA activity is most often assessed using cortisol, a steroid hormone produced by the HPA axis, with high levels of cortisol (i.e., hypercortisolism) corresponding to high levels of HPA activity (i.e., HPA hyperactivity). Adult studies of cortisol–depression links have demonstrated that adults with depression show higher basal (i.e., resting) levels of cortisol (Stetler & Miller, 2011), blunted cortisol reactivity in response to psychological stressors (Burke et al., 2005), and elevated levels of cortisol during recovery (Burke et al., 2005).

Downward extensions of this work to children have similarly indicated that higher basal levels of cortisol distinguish children with and without depression and that the size of this difference increases with age (Guerry & Hastings, 2011; Kaufman et al., 2001). Considerably fewer studies have examined whether changes in HPA activity in response to psychosocial stressors (i.e., HPA reactivity) likewise differentiates those with and without depression, especially among children aged twelve years and younger. Preliminary evidence indicates that links between cortisol reactivity and depression also change as a function of development (Burke et al., 2005; Lopez-Duran et al., 2009), with blunted cortisol reactivity showing associations with depression in childhood (Hankin et al., 2010; Luby et al., 2003; Suzuki et al., 2013) but, conversely, elevated cortisol reactivity showing associations with depression in postpubescent children (e.g., Gong et al., 2019; Hankin et al., 2010; Lopez-Duran et al., 2015). Importantly, most research to date investigating links between cortisol and depression has been cross-sectional and therefore provides limited information about whether HPA dysregulation *precedes* the onset of depression or vice versa. Nevertheless, some evidence suggests that greater increases in cortisol across development may precede the onset of depression in adolescence and early adulthood (e.g., Adam et al., 2010; Carnegie et al., 2014).

Research considering PNS dysregulation as a biomarker of childhood depression also arose from the adult literature. PNS activity is most often indexed by high-frequency heart rate variability (HF-HRV) or respiratory sinus arrhythmia (RSA), which are synonymous and which capture the influence of the PNS on the heart. In parallel to findings that have emerged in adult literature, in a meta-analysis that investigated differences in basal HF-HRV among children with and without depression, Koenig and colleagues (2016) found moderately strong group differences between children with and without depression, such that children with depression showed significantly lower basal HF-HRV. However, in contrast to adult literature (Kemp et al., 2010), levels of HF-HRV did not show inverse associations with depression severity (Koenig et al., 2016).

In a qualitative review that investigated associations between changes in HF-HRV in response to psychosocial stressors (i.e., HF-HRV reactivity) and depression across the lifespan, Hamilton and Alloy (2016) reported that children with depression consistently showed dysregulated patterns of HF-HRV reactivity.

However, the direction of HF-HRV dysregulation was unclear, with some studies indicating that children with depression exhibit greater HF-HRV reactivity (i.e., greater decreases in HF-HRV) and others indicating that children with depression showed blunted HF-HRV reactivity (i.e., smaller decreases in HF-HRV). The authors speculated that these complex associations could reflect heterogeneity in the pathophysiology underlying depression, measurement issues (e.g., differences in basal HF-HRV), or the possible presence of other moderating influences (e.g., activities of other stress response subsystems, stress exposure). Of importance, similar to studies investigating HPA–depression linkages, most studies to date investigating PNS–depression associations in children have been cross-sectional in nature, although not all (Bosch et al., 2009; Pang & Beauchaine, 2013). Finally, HF-HRV has been identified as a transdiagnostic indicator of risk for a range of mental health problems (Beauchaine, 2015; Beauchaine & Thayer, 2015) and thus is not specific to depression.

Much less work has investigated whether SNS dysregulation also shows associations with childhood depression, though some evidence suggests that SNS dysregulation may also be tied to internalizing disorders (Boyce et al., 2001; Jones et al., 2020; Weems et al., 2005). However, similar to studies considering links between PNS activity and depression, both SNS excess and blunted responsivity have shown associations with internalizing problems such as depression. Finally, several scholars have now underscored the importance of considering the unique contributions of each stress response subsystem (i.e., HPA, PNS, and SNS) to the development of psychopathology and how they contribute collectively (Bauer et al., 2002; Berntson et al., 1994; Del Giudice et al., 2011). Thus, one potentially promising avenue of research may be to clarify the ways in which coordinated *patterns* of stress responsivity across HPA, PNS, and SNS subsystems underlie the development of childhood depression.

5.1.2.2 Neural Connectivity

Neuroimaging studies of childhood depression remain a nascent but rapidly growing area of research, with nearly all human studies emerging only within the last two decades and all longitudinal human studies within the last decade. Early cross-sectional neuroimaging work yielded convincing findings that were complementary to adult neuroimaging studies (Davidson et al., 2009; Hulvershorn et al., 2011). These findings suggested that children who had or were at risk for depression showed corticolimbic abnormalities, such as among brain regions associated with affective (e.g., the amygdala) and cognitive processes (e.g., the prefrontal cortex) involved in emotion processing and regulation. However, emergent qualitative and quantitative reviews of longitudinal neuroimaging work have drawn focal attention to differences with reward processing secondary to striatal abnormalities (Keren et al., 2018; Luking et al., 2016; Toenders et al., 2019). Furthermore, a meta-analysis of sixty-eight longitudinal neuroimaging studies suggested that this shift in attention may be well justified. Specifically, Toenders and colleagues (2019) found that, although some evidence supported the notion that blunted neural responsivity in the corticolimbic regions precedes the onset of depression or increases in depressive symptoms, blunted neural responsivity in the ventral striatum during reward processing tasks appeared to be the most robust neuroimaging biomarker of pediatric depression. Importantly, although this pattern of blunted reward responsivity has emerged in samples of children as young as five years old (Belden et al., 2015), only a small minority of studies that have been completed to date has focused on samples of children aged twelve or younger (Toenders et al., 2019). Thus, further clarification about the extent to which these premorbid neural indices of risk are consistent across development is needed before firm conclusions may be reliably drawn.

5.1.3 Temperament

Temperament represents individual differences in children's proclivities for reactivity and regulation (Rothbart, 2011). Temperament has bases in genetics but continues to transact with biological and environmental factors throughout childhood to form the basis for adult personality. Factor analyses of children's temperament characteristics have yielded three broad factors that emerge consistently across cultures: negative emotionality, surgency/extraversion, and effortful control (Gartstein & Rothbart, 2003; Putnam et al., 2006; Rothbart et al., 2001). *Negative emotionality* characterizes proclivities to experience negative mood, including sadness, fear, anger, and discomfort. Children who are high in negative emotionality tend to experience negative mood intensely and frequently and accordingly are more likely to perceive stressful life events as distressing compared to their low negative emotionality counterparts (Lengua & Long, 2002; Mezulis et al., 2006). *Surgency/extraversion* characterizes proclivities for positive affect, strong approach and reward motivation, and sensation seeking. Children who are high in surgency tend to smile and laugh often, to be active and exploratory, and to enjoy highly stimulating activities like rough and tumble play. *Effortful control* characterizes proclivities for regulation and soothability, task persistence, and enjoyment of low-intensity activities. Children who are high in effortful control tend to manage their attention and behavior easily, recover easily from stress and distress, sit and stay focused for extended periods of time, persist with challenging activities, and enjoy low-stimulation activities like reading and quiet play. Each of these temperament factors has shown connections to childhood depression.

Among temperament factors, high negative emotionality has consistently emerged as a robust vulnerability characteristic for the development of depression, especially when coupled with low surgency (especially low positive affect) and low effortful control (Dougherty et al., 2010; Kotelnikova et al., 2015; Reinfjell et al., 2016; van Beveren et al., 2019). These associations show consistency with clinical models of personality and depression that suggest that trait-like tendencies for negative affect and low positive affect appear to heighten risk for depression, that is, the tripartite model of anxiety and depression (Anderson & Hope, 2008; De Bolle & De Fruyt, 2010). Furthermore, these temperament–depression risk associations have been replicated across cultures (Austin & Chorpita, 2004) and may be universal; however, see the discussion in Section 5.1.3.2 in regard to sociocultural considerations. Of note, high negative emotionality and low effortful control are each believed to confer transdiagnostic risk for psychopathology in general and are not necessarily unique to the incidence of depression in children (Aldao et al., 2016; Beauchaine & Tackett, 2020; Hankin et al., 2017).

5.1.3.1 Explanatory Models Linking Temperament with Depression

Several models for understanding temperamental risk for psychopathology have been proposed (Clark et al., 1994; Nigg, 2006). *Spectrum* or *continuity models* view temperament and psychopathology as related constructs that sit on the same continuum and accordingly posit that psychopathology merely reflects extreme manifestations of certain temperament characteristics. Consistent with this conceptualization, there are ostensible parallels between various temperament characteristics and depressive symptomatology, such as between high negative emotionality and sad moods or negative cognitions; low positive affect and low approach (components of surgency) and anhedonia; and poor attentional control (a component of effortful control) and difficulty concentrating (Compas et al., 2004). Likewise, items assessing temperament and internalizing distress on parent and self-report inventories have been found to overlap substantially (Lemery et al., 2002), further underscoring the notion that the two constructs may be difficult to disentangle.

Behavioral genetic studies have also yielded support for the notion that components of temperament – especially negative emotionality – and depression may share common genetic bases (Gjone & Stevenson, 1997; Neiss et al.,

2009). Nevertheless, on the whole, temperament and psychopathology tend to share less variance than would be expected if they were fully overlapping constructs (Nigg, 2006). Thus, their common etiological bases only account for a limited portion of their relations.

Susceptibility or *pathoplasty* models predominate in the literature considering links between temperament and psychopathology and broadly encompass diathesis–stress (Monroe & Simons,1991; Sameroff, 1983), differential susceptibility (Belsky & Pluess, 2009; Ellis et al., 2011), and pathoplasty models (Clark et al., 1994). Although distinct, these models share the perspective that temperament alone does not *cause* depression, as is held by spectrum models, but that some temperament characteristics increase the likelihood that children will develop depression especially in the presence of other risk factors. Stated differently, these temperament characteristics exacerbate or mitigate the adverse effects of other risk processes. In line with this assertion, a number of studies have yielded support for the notion that a child's temperament may influence the likelihood that exposure to other risk factors will precipitate internalizing distress including depressive symptoms (Hastings et al., 2015; Lewis & Olsson, 2011; Pitzer et al., 2017).

Finally, *programming* or *scar* models represent a promising perspective for understanding links between temperament and psychopathology. Programming models (e.g., Gluckman & Hanson, 2006; Pluess & Belsky, 2011) posit that early life stress may prompt the recalibration of psychobiological systems in ways that "program" enduring functional risk for psychopathology. Similarly, scar models (e.g., Lewinsohn et al., 1981) posit that early pathological experiences (e.g., of depression) permanently "scar" temperament or personality in ways that heighten risk for subsequent psychopathology. Programming and scar models have not typically been grouped together, yet they and other similar models, such as adaptive calibration (Del Giudice et al., 2011) and enduring effect models (Fraley et al., 2013), converge in their suggestions that experiences of stress and distress result in enduring changes to emotion reactivity and regulation in ways that maintain or potentiate future psychopathology, such as depressive disorders. There is now some agreement that exposure to stress during pregnancy and the early postpartum may shape child temperament (Gartstein & Skinner, 2018; Huizink, 2008), with prenatal stress showing consistent, albeit modest, links with negative emotionality and regulatory difficulties (Hartman & Belsky, 2018; Korja et al., 2017). Furthermore, some evidence suggests that these enduring alterations to temperament and personality may likewise occur as a result of exposure to childhood stress (Hopkins et al., 2013; Kiff et al., 2011) and distress (Davies & Windle, 2001; Shiner et al., 2002).

5.1.3.2 Developmental Processes Linking Temperament with Depression

The developmental processes underlying links between temperament and depression are complex and unfold as a result of any number of multifaceted transactions with genetic, biological, contextual, and other influences. In the context of these transactions, temperament may be viewed as exerting direct, indirect, and interactive effects on depression (Clark et al., 1994; Nigg, 2006). For example, as discussed in Section 5.1.3, temperament may contribute to depression directly by predisposing children to higher baseline levels and frequency of irritable, anhedonic, and sad moods. Temperament may also increase the incidence of maladaptive cognitions and behaviors that are tied to depression (Hankin et al., 2009). For example, in a study of nine-to-twelve-year-old children of divorce, Lengua and Long (2002) found that children who were higher in negative emotionality perceived stressful life events as more threatening and that threat perceptions in turn were associated with elevated depressive symptoms. Similarly, Hayden and colleagues (2006) found that children who were lower in positive emotionality at age three were less likely to make positive self-statements compared to their higher positive emotionality counterparts and were also observed to give up more easily during a challenging task. These cognitions and behaviors may in turn generate more stress while also increasing vulnerability to those stressors (Hammen, 2005; Hankin et al., 2009; see also Section 5.1.4 for a discussion about social-cognitive vulnerability factors).

Temperament may also contribute to the development of depression indirectly, such as by influencing how caregivers, siblings, and peers respond to children in ways that heighten or mitigate risk for depression (see Sections 5.3 and 5.4 for a discussion of parent and peer risk processes). Perhaps most intuitively, high negative emotionality elicits more ineffective and harsh parenting behaviors (Bates et al., 2012), as well as lower teacher and peer ratings of social competence (Eisenberg et al., 2001; Sallquist et al., 2010). Similarly, some evidence suggests that low surgency (Kochanska et al., 2004; Wetter & Hankin, 2009) and low effortful control may undermine the quality of interpersonal relationships (Bates et al., 2012; Zhou et al., 2010). Thus, temperament characteristics may shape the environment in ways that heighten risk for child maladaptation in general and depression in particular.

Importantly, the nature of these evocative effects is known to vary across cultures in ways that likely reflect the goodness of fit between various child characteristics and broader cultural values (Berdan et al., 2008; Bornstein & Cote, 2009). In a study that considered parent perceptions of temperament across seven Western countries, Super and colleagues (2008) found that the child characteristics parents perceived to be challenging differed across countries. Similarly, in a study that compared associations between temperament and teacher ratings of adjustment in the United States and China, Zhou and colleagues (2009) found that teachers were more likely to rate children who were high in positive emotionality as maladjusted in China but not in the United States. Finally, the extent to which certain temperament traits are perceived as desirable or undesirable may further vary *within* cultures as a function of sociodemographic factors like gender (e.g., Berdan et al., 2008). For example, temperamental shyness has been found to be especially problematic for boys in Western societies (Coplan et al., 2001; Gazelle & Ladd, 2003) and is believed to reflect the impact of gendered cultural expectations for greater assertiveness and approach orientation in boys and men (Rubin & Coplan, 2007). As such, conceptualizations of the role of child evocative effects on adjustment are incomplete without acknowledgment of their context within broader sociocultural systems.

Last, temperament may contribute to the development of depression interactively, such as by amplifying the adverse effects of other internal or external risk factors. In recognizing the dynamic interplay of temperament with the environment, Chess and Thomas (1999) – pioneers of temperament research – underscored the importance of considering the "goodness of fit" of child temperament with the demands, expectations, and opportunities of the environment. For example, in considering the evocative effects of certain "difficult" temperament characteristics as previously described, Chess and Thomas observed that whether these evocative effects occur often depends as much on caregivers' behaviors and characteristics as children's (Chess & Thomas, 1999; Kiff et al., 2011).

On the caregiver side, some caregivers may be more averse to child fussing and whining due to their own temperament characteristics, cultural values, or for some other reason (Mäntymaa et al., 2006; Wilson & Durbin, 2010). On the child side, children who are high in negative emotionality such as irritability and sadness may perceive and react to mildly critical parenting in more intense ways thereby magnifying ostensible adverse outcomes associated with external stressors (Oldehinkel et al., 2006). These interactive processes appear to be especially relevant for children who are high in negative emotionality, especially during infancy (Kiff et al., 2011; Slagt et al., 2016), with clear implications for the emergence of depressive symptoms.

5.1.4 Social-Cognitive Influences

Cogito, ergo sum (I think, therefore I am). Rene Descartes famously highlighted the centrality of cognitions to humans' existence as well as the salience of perceptions for shaping individuals' subjective realities. Insofar as cognitions literally define the ways in which we perceive and make sense of the world, it is unsurprising that cognitive theories of depression represent some of the most prominent etiological models for understanding the emergence of depression in adults. In fact, all the cognitive vulnerability factors for childhood depression that have received research attention were cognitive vulnerability factors that first gained prominence in research with adults. Research that has extended cognitive theories of adult depression to child depression suggests that the same cognitive vulnerability factors confer risk for childhood depression beginning as early as age eight (Abela & Hankin, 2008; Jacobs et al., 2008; Lakdawalla et al., 2007), if not earlier (i.e., age five; Conley et al., 2001). Specifically, negative attributional biases, dysfunctional attitudes, and ruminative cognitive styles have each been implicated in the onset, maintenance, and recurrence of childhood depression.

Conceptualizations about the role of each of these maladaptive cognitions stem from distinct theoretical models. Interest in *negative attributional biases* stems from Abramson and colleagues' (1995) hopelessness theory of depression, which represents one of the most studied cognitive theories of depression in children (Abela & Hankin, 2008; Jacobs et al., 2008). According to the hopelessness theory of depression, individuals' tendencies to attribute negative events to global and stable causes (e.g., "I failed the exam because I am not smart enough"), perceive negative events as having disastrous consequences (e.g., "I will probably flunk out of school"), and experience low self-efficacy in the aftermath of negative life events (e.g., "There is nothing I can do to change this trajectory") can engender hopelessness and, consequentially, depression.

The focus on *dysfunctional attitudes* arises from Beck's (2008) cognitive theory, which posits that individuals who ascribe to depressogenic schema, or maladaptive core beliefs, are more likely to engage in thinking errors about the self (e.g., "I am a failure"), the world (e.g., "If I do not do well in school, then I am a failure as a person"), and the future (e.g., "I will never be good at anything") and that these thinking errors collectively precipitate the development of depression.

Finally, work considering *ruminative cognitive styles* emerges from Nolen-Hoeksema's (2004) response styles theory. Response styles theory postulates that individuals with ruminative response styles, characterized as repetitive and passive thoughts pertaining to depressive symptomatology (e.g., "Why can't I focus on my schoolwork? What's wrong with me?"), are more likely to experience increases in both the frequency and the severity of depressive symptoms over time.

Importantly, the contributions of these cognitive factors to depression are small overall, especially before the age of twelve (Lakdawalla et al., 2007). Some scholars have posited that the smaller effect sizes observed in childhood versus adolescent or adult depression may reflect differences in children's cognitive developmental capabilities. For example, Cole and Turner (1993) posited that cognitive vulnerabilities may contribute minimally to risk for depression until children develop the capacity for abstract reasoning, such as is necessary to infer causation, which typically begins in late childhood and early adolescence. Similarly, Gibb and Coles (2005) pointed out that children's capacities to make stable, internal attributions about the causes of events (e.g., to personal failures) increases gradually across development in parallel with cognitive maturational processes (e.g., development of self-concept, theory of mind, autobiographical memory). Nevertheless, other scholars have cautioned that apparent differences in effect sizes linking cognitive vulnerability factors to depression in childhood versus adolescence and adulthood may also reflect methodological challenges with assessing cognitions earlier compared to later in childhood (Hankin & Abela, 2005; Lakdawalla et al., 2007). Thus, more developmentally informed research that employs rigorous assessments of children's cognitions is warranted before definitive conclusions about developmentally based differences in cognition–depression linkages can be drawn. Similarly, there is some preliminary evidence that the nature or prominence of maladaptive cognitions that underlie depression may differ across cultures but that they nonetheless play a similar role in the ontogeny of depression across cultures (Auerbach et al., 2010; Calvete et al., 2008; Rooney et al., 2013). Nonetheless, whether and how cultural influences may shape the links between cognitions and children's depressive experience remains vastly underexplored.

Of note, maladaptive cognitions themselves are believed to emerge as a result of genetics; temperament; parent, peer, and interpersonal processes; and stressful life events (Hankin et al., 2009). Thus, maladaptive cognitions appear to represent one common mechanism through which these other risk factors may heighten children's vulnerability for depression. As such, it is unsurprising that interventions targeting these maladaptive cognitions have emerged as one of the premier treatments for depression in children, adolescents, and adults alike (see Section 7 for a discussion of empirically supported interventions). Last, despite origins in theories of depression, these cognitive vulnerability factors have been implicated more broadly as transdiagnostic vulnerability factors that increase risk for a range of mental health conditions and do not appear to be unique to depression (Hankin et al., 2016).

5.1.5 Explanatory Models Linking Maladaptive Cognitions with Depression

In contrast to explanatory models linking temperament with depression, maladaptive cognitions are widely regarded to represent susceptibility factors and, more specifically, diatheses that increase the vulnerability for depression *among children with significant stress exposure*. In other words, as is the case for other vulnerability factors that have been implicated in the development of depression, maladaptive cognitions are believed to increase the probability that stress and adversity will result in depression but do not themselves provide sufficient explanatory power for the development of depression. Some evidence also suggests that scar models, in which earlier episodes of psychopathology alter cognitions in relatively enduring ways, may also apply (Hankin et al., 2016). Nevertheless, neither the diathesis–stress nor scar models explain how maladaptive cognitions independently or collectively contribute to depression.

Three prominent models that consider the interrelations among maladaptive cognitions attempt to offer some explanations: the multiplicative approach; the additive approach; and the weakest link approach (Abela & Hankin, 2008; Abela & Sarin, 2002). The *multiplicative approach* proposes that maladaptive cognitions interact synergistically to heighten vulnerability for depression, such that individuals with multiple cognitive vulnerability factors are viewed to be at greatest risk for depression. Because it is conceptually and statistically challenging to model synergistic interactions involving more than two cognitive vulnerability factors, most research adopting a multiplicative approach has tested whether risk associated with a given maladaptive cognition (e.g., negative attributional style) is compounded by the presence of another maladaptive cognition (e.g., negative self-concept). Similar to the multiplicative approach, the *additive approach* suggests that an individual's degree of vulnerability for depression depends on the sum of their vulnerability and protective factors. For example, in this model, children who exhibit three maladaptive cognitions (e.g., negative attributional style, negative self-concept, ruminative tendencies) would be more likely to develop depression than children who exhibited only one of those maladaptive cognitions (e.g., negative attributional style, average self-concept, average rumination) or children who exhibited more protective cognitions (e.g., negative attributional style, high positive self-concept, low rumination). The *weakest link approach* proposes that an individual's degree of susceptibility for depression depends on the degree of susceptibility conferred by their most maladaptive cognition (i.e., their "weakest link").

Some support has emerged for each of these three models, albeit to differing degrees and under different circumstances (Abela & Hankin, 2008). For example, Hankin and colleagues (2016) speculated that the relevance of these models may differ across development. Specifically, Hankin and colleagues found that maladaptive cognitions appear to be relatively independent earlier in childhood but become integrated during the transition from childhood to adolescence (Adams et al., 2007; Hankin et al., 2007). Correspondingly, they proposed that a weakest link model may be more relevant during early and middle childhood when cognitions remain more distinct from one another but that an additive or multiplicative model may fit better by adolescence once cognitions become more closely interrelated (Hankin et al., 2016). However, no empirical studies to our knowledge have tested these developmental hypotheses to date.

5.2 Stress Contexts and Adverse Life Events

Substantial theoretical and empirical work has underscored the centrality of stress and adversity to the development of psychopathology (Grant et al., 2004). In fact, exposure to stress and adversity has been found to increase risk for major depressive disorder by as much as two- to threefold in children and adolescents (LeMoult et al., 2020). Despite its salience, stress as a construct has remained elusive and has been challenging to define across decades of research (e.g., Cohen et al., 1995; Doom & Cicchetti, 2018). Much of this difficulty is owed to the breadth of the construct as it has been operationalized, with stressors variously operationalized as comprising the psychosocial, environmental, and physical; subjective and objective; minor, major, adverse, and traumatic; episodic, intermittent, and chronic; and direct and vicarious – to name a few. Furthermore, it is notable that, because few stressors occur in isolation (e.g., poverty, malnutrition, exposure to neighborhood violence, and parent mental illness often co-occur), it is exceedingly difficult (and, in most cases, of limited practical value) to parse the discrete contributions of any one stressor (Doom & Cicchetti, 2018; Evans et al., 2013). Given the challenges inherent in stress research, it is easy to see why broad-based indices of cumulative risk exposure (e.g., stressful life events, adverse childhood experiences), which typically span an array of stressors and adverse experiences, have generated a great deal of interest and attention (Evans et al., 2013). This work has yielded important insights about stress–psychopathology associations, especially to underscore the insidious consequences of multiple risk exposure for long-term health and well-being (Evans et al., 2013; McLaughlin, 2016). At the same time, the reliance on the summation of stressors without consideration for similarities or differences between the types, severity, or chronicity of constituent stressors makes this literature difficult to interpret.

As a case in point, it is notable that the oft-cited and widely used construct of "adverse childhood experiences" has been used to describe everything from child abuse and neglect to experiences of racism and discrimination and to poor academic performance (Evans et al., 2013; Finkelhor et al., 2013). At the risk of implying that chronic, low acuity stressors do not have insidious consequences for long-term health and well-being – many do (a point we elaborate on further in Section 5.5) – the mechanisms and risk processes that link disparate forms of stress with adjustment are likely distinct (Grant et al., 2003; McLaughlin & Sheridan, 2016). As such, scholars have highlighted a need for greater differentiation among distinct forms of stress in ways that are conceptually meaningful, such as by identifying taxonomies or dimensions of stress that may have unique implications for emotional development (Doyle & Cicchetti, 2018; Grant et al., 2004; McLaughlin & Sheridan, 2016) and, by implication, depressive experience in childhood.

For example, building on the work of Nolen-Hoeksema and Watkins (2011), McLaughlin and Sheridan (2016) proposed a dimensional model of childhood adversity that distinguishes between stressors by way of their differential associations with various transdiagnostic risk mechanisms (Figure 1).

Specifically, they posited that it may be to useful to differentiate between stressors that invoke threat (i.e., of harm – for example, exposure to or violent victimization) and those stressors that invoke deprivation (i.e., of expected environmental stimulation and input – for example, neglect or poverty) given evidence that experiences of threat may be uniquely associated with aberrant fear learning and contrastingly that experiences of deprivation may be uniquely associated with disturbances with reward learning and executive

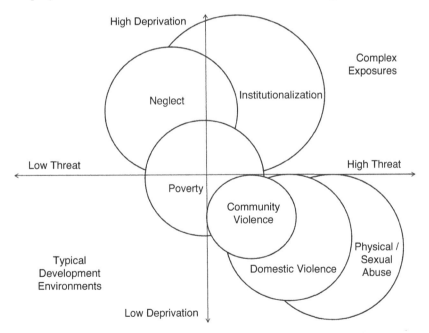

Figure 1 Dimensional model of childhood adversity

Note: Examples of commonly studied forms of adversity are placed along central dimensions of threat and deprivation. Larger circles indicate greater variance in the degree to which the experience reflects the underlying dimension. From "Beyond Cumulative Risk: A Dimensional Approach to Childhood Adversity," by K. A. McLaughlin and M. A. Sheridan, 2016, *Current Directions in Psychological Science*, 24(4), p. 241. Copyright K. A. McLaughlin & M. A. Sheridan.

functions. Drawing from evolutionary-developmental perspectives, Del Giudice and colleagues (2011) proposed the *adaptive calibration model* (Figure 2 and Table 2), which theorizes that exposure to varying degrees of stress during sensitive periods of development – or developmental "switch points" – may alter the stress response system in ways that have enduring consequences for later adjustment. Specifically, they proposed that four prototypical profiles of physiological stress responsivity may emerge in response to low, moderate, high, and extreme levels of stress exposure. In turn, each profile is associated with distinct patterns of emotional and behavioral responding that confer evolutionary adaptation; that is, they promote survival and reproduction in the stress contexts where they arise even if they may not do so in the broader societal context.

Promising preliminary support has emerged for this model (Del Giudice et al., 2012; Ellis et al., 2017; Lin et al., 2020), yet much room remains for empirical vetting and elaboration. Beyond the ways in which stressful life experiences can directly impact children's development, stressful life experiences may also contribute by invoking risk processes in children's more proximal family context, which we discuss next.

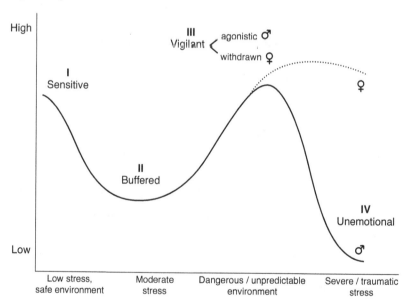

Figure 2 The adaptive calibration model of individual differences in development of stress responsivity

Note: From "The Adaptative Calibration Model of stress responsivity," by M. Del Giudice, B. J. Ellis, E. A., Shirtcliff, 2011, *Neuroscience & Biobehavioral Reviews*, 7, p. 1577. Reprinted with permission.

Table 2 Summary of predictions by the adaptive calibration model

ACM pattern	Early environment	Putative responsivity to environmental influence	Social and behavioral correlates/LH strategy
Sensitive	Low stress, safe environment	High	Slow LH strategy: reflective; self- and other-conscious; high inhibitory control; socially cooperative
Buffered	Moderate stress	Moderate to Low	Slow LH strategy: low anxiety, aggression, and risk-taking/risk-seeking behavior; socially oriented
Vigilant	High stress, unpredictable environment	High	Fast LH strategy: – *Withdrawn* (♀) – high trait anxiety and hypervigilance; high rejection sensitivity – *Agonistic* (♂) – high risk-taking; impulsive; socially competitive; social aggression; low cooperation
Unemotional	Severe/traumatic stress	Low*	Fast LH strategy: – ♂ – Low empathy and cooperation; impulsive; competitive risk-taking, more antisocial behaviors, more callous–unemotional traits – ♀ – Reduced social cooperation/social orientation

Note. *blunted physiological responsivity to performance-related stressors and social evaluation but autonomic activation during agonistic encounters.
ACM = adaptive calibration model; LH = life history.
Source. From Lin et al. (2021, p. 209).

5.3 Family–Parent–Intergenerational Transmission

As noted in Section 5.1.1, parent depression is one of the most prominent risk factors for childhood depression and, at least before adolescence, appears to exert influence primarily by way of social and contextual rather than genetic transmission processes (Hannigan et al., 2018). Furthermore, evidence suggests that these risk associations extend beyond exposure to parent depression to more broadly comprise exposure to parent stress likely due in part to the interrelatedness of stress and depression. These processes begin to unfold with exposures that occur before birth with the maternal intrauterine environment representing the foremost environment to which children are exposed and extend to exposures that occur in infancy and beyond. In this section, we review research that addresses the factors and processes by which parents and parenting influence the development of depressive experience in children.

5.3.1 Prenatal Maternal Contexts and Fetal Programming

Experts agree that parent experiences of stress and distress likely begin to influence children's susceptibility for depression, among other emotional and behavioral problems, before birth (Gartstein & Skinner, 2018; Schlotz & Phillips, 2009). A number of studies have linked maternal stress and distress during pregnancy with several child vulnerability factors that are in turn linked to childhood depression, including temperamental negative emotionality and biological stress reactivity (Lin et al., 2017; Van den Bergh et al., 2017). Additionally, evidence from animal studies suggests that fetal exposure to maternal stress also results in neurological abnormalities in the striatal area (Bonapersona et al., 2018), which underlies reward processing, a function that has demonstrated strong relations to depression in childhood (Vidal-Ribas et al., 2019). These associations are theorized to emerge as a result of *fetal programming*, in which exposure to maternal stress during pregnancy alters offspring neurobiological systems in ways that have enduring consequences for future health and well-being (Barker, 2007; Gluckman & Hanson, 2006). Furthermore, an emerging line of research suggests that intrauterine stress exposure may involve maternal stressors that occur during pregnancy and maternal *preconception* stressors that women have experienced across the life course (Gray et al., 2017; Scorza et al., 2018). For example, maternal childhood histories of trauma have been linked to infants' low birthweight (Scorza et al., 2018), which is believed correspond with alterations to infant neurobiological systems that underlie stress reactivity (i.e., HPA and ANS reactivity; Glover & Hill, 2012; O'Donnell & Meaney, 2017).

Although the exact mechanisms that underlie fetal programming are unknown, exposure to maternal excess glucocorticoids during periods of rapid fetal development is believed to prompt fetal neurobiological systems to make homeostatic adjustments (Barker, 2007; Gluckman & Hanson, 2006). Notably, glucocorticoid production naturally decreases during pregnancy. Thus, the pathophysiology of excess glucocorticoid production may follow multiple pathways, including exposure to intense or chronic stress, such as in the case of prenatal stress exposure, HPA dysregulation, or heightened transplacental passage of glucocorticoids via placental dysregulation (O'Donnell et al., 2012). These homeostatic adjustments likely occur as a result of epigenetic processes through which environmental exposures influence gene expression (Hochberg et al., 2011).

The nature of these homeostatic adjustments appears to differ for female compared to male fetuses, with female fetuses more likely to show growth restriction and heightened HPA reactivity in response to intrauterine stress exposure (Carpenter et al., 2017; Glover & Hill, 2012; Sandman et al., 2013). In contrast, male fetuses follow typical rates of physical development but are more likely to terminate or to show immature neuromuscular development at birth (Glover & Hill, 2012; Sandman et al., 2013). These sex differences are believed in turn to render girls more susceptible to subsequent experiences of stress and may contribute in part to the developmental processes across childhood that lead to higher rates of depression observed among adolescent girls and women (Sandman et al., 2013).

5.3.2 Postnatal Family Contexts and Parent–Infant Transactions

Exposure to postnatal stress and distress during infancy likewise heightens vulnerability for childhood depression by influencing infants' developing regulatory systems (Field, 1994; Hendrix et al., 2018). This exposure is believed to reflect the impact of parents' stress and distress on parents' capacities to engage in the sensitive, synchronous, and reciprocal coregulatory interactions that support infant regulatory capacity (Field, 1994, 1995; Tronick & Reck, 2009). That is, because infancy is a period of rapid neurobiological development, infants' maturing neurobiological systems are highly plastic to environmental influences. Furthermore, because infants are born almost, if not entirely, dependent on caregiver coregulatory behaviors to meet basic needs like feeding, sleeping, and temperature regulation, caregiver coregulatory behaviors that regularly and consistently meet infants' physiological needs are believed to scaffold more consistent and rhythmic patterns of physiological regulation in ways that support regulatory development (Bornstein, 2013).

In fact, contingent and responsive caregiver behaviors precede more state regulation beginning as early as the first ten days of life. In a powerful early study that compared newborns receiving regularly scheduled care (e.g., feeding, diaper changes, social interaction) with newborns receiving responsive care (i.e., according to infant cues), Sander et al. (1972) found that infants receiving responsive care developed more regular patterns of sleeping, feeding, and elimination compared to their counterparts receiving routine care. When extended across infancy, the external regulatory supports afforded by inter-actions with responsive and synchronous caregivers are essentially internalized and promote infants' and toddlers' increasing capacities to regulate internal physiological states, including those that support emotional and behavioral regulation.

The consequences of parent stress and distress for infant regulatory and subsequent socioemotional development have often been exemplified in studies of maternal depression. Consistent with the notion that the consequences extend broadly to stress and distress, maternal depression appears to exert a dose-response effect on infant development, with the strength of associations more closely linked to the presence of depressive symptoms than on clinical diagno-ses alone (Goodman et al., 2011; Weinberg et al., 2001). This dose-response effect is believed to further reflect the impact of maternal stress and distress on the severity and chronicity of functional impairment as it impacts mothers' emotional availability during formative mother–infant interactions through which infants first learn to regulate their emotions and behaviors (Weinberg et al., 2001).

Tronick proposed a mutual regulation model of parent–infant interaction in which parents and infants can optimally modulate their own affect and behav-iors to achieve a state of mutual regulation that can be thought of as an interpersonal state of intimacy, connectedness, or mutual enjoyment (Tronick, 2007). Tronick (2007) described the dynamic process of achieving mutual regulation as a dance in which parents and infants strive to take coordinated steps together and has underscored that *how* parents and infants function together as dance partners is as important for shaping infants' emotional and behavioral regulation, if not more so, than how beautiful their dance is. Parent–infant dyads that communicate effectively ultimately support states of mutual regulation and, accordingly, of infant regulation, whereas parent–infant dyads that communicate ineffectively may heighten states of dyadic dysregulation and, in turn, of infant dysregulation.

Parent depression can undermine parental capacities to support reciprocal and synchronous patterns of engagement such as by disrupting parent abilities to notice and respond effectively to infant cues. Parent depression may also interfere with parent capacities to regulate their own emotions and behaviors in ways that sustain synchronous interactions or promote repair from mismatched interactions. Indeed, mothers with depression have repeatedly shown more incongruent affect (e.g., sad or flat affect) and behaviors (e.g., inattention), initiate fewer touching behaviors, and engage in less sensitive parenting behaviors during mother–infant interactions compared to mothers without depression (Bernard et al., 2018; Tronick & Reck, 2009). Even brief disruptions to mothers' emotional availability, such as those simulated in experimental manipulations of parent depressed affect (e.g., still-face paradigm; Tronick et al., 1978), have been found to elicit signs of infant emotional (e.g., negative affect) and behavioral (e.g., gaze aversion, self-comforting, banging, and back arching) distress (Manian & Bornstein, 2009; Mesman et al., 2009; Weinberg & Tronick, 1996). When extended over the course of repeated interactions, infants are believed to internalize these negative states such as by showing increases in dispositional proclivities for negative affectivity (Braungart-Rieker et al., 2010) and ultimately to further amplify the prominence of dyadic dysregulation that can eventually promote depressive experience.

5.3.3 Family Transactions in the Toddler Years and Beyond

By the time a child has reached toddler and early childhood years, warm and sensitive parenting continues to buffer against risk for childhood depression. However, harsh and rejecting parenting emerges as a more prominent risk mechanism through which parent and family stress may contribute to childhood depression (Dallaire et al., 2006). Harsh and rejecting parenting has been found to account for the effects of parent psychopathology and children's adjustment and for other prominent family stressors including parent marital conflict, divorce, and separation (Grant et al., 2006). Additionally, harsh and rejecting parenting is believed to represent a key mediator of more distal, socioecological stressors such as economic hardship, neighborhood quality, and socioecological disadvantage (Barajas-Gonzalez & Brooks-Gunn, 2014; Conger et al., 2002; Vreeland et al., 2019).

The notion that parental harshness and rejection figures more prominently in risk for childhood depression than parental warmth and sensitivity lends insight into the drivers of risk in childhood. Specifically and importantly, harsh and rejecting versus warm and sensitive parenting practices are orthogonal constructs (Dallaire et al., 2006; Grusec & Davidov, 2010) and are believed to contribute to different aspects of children's emotion socialization. In childhood, parental warmth and sensitivity contribute more prominently to the regulation of positive emotion and, relatedly, to children's social competence (Davidov &

Grusec, 2006; Moran et al., 2019) as well as to children's use of constructive coping strategies (Valiente et al., 2004). In contrast, parental harshness and rejection are related to increased negative affect as well as to difficulties with negative emotion expression and regulation (Chang et al., 2003; Scaramella & Leve, 2004), qualities associated with the development of depressive symptoms.

Consistent with this suggestion, Luebbe and Bell (2014) found that mothers' low warmth (i.e., acceptance and positive emotion expressiveness) and high harsh parenting behaviors (i.e., psychological control and negative emotion expressiveness) were both associated with children's depression in a sample of twelve-to-fifteen-year-olds but that they appeared to operate through distinct mechanisms. Specifically, warm parenting appeared to confer risk for depression through children's low positive affect, whereas harsh parenting appeared to confer risk through children's high negative affect. Importantly, these data were cross-sectional and thus preclude the capacity to test true temporal relations. Nevertheless, these findings further dovetail with insights from temperament literature, which, as discussed in Section 5.1.3, implicates negative emotionality and, to a lesser but nonetheless significant extent, low positive emotionality as risk factors underlying childhood depression. Furthermore, they shed light on a potentially promising avenue for clarifying both equifinality (e.g., of distinct subtypes of childhood depression) and multifinality (e.g., of distinct developmental pathways to childhood depression) in childhood depression.

In terms of underlying developmental processes, Morris and colleagues (2007) proposed a tripartite model of familial influence on children's emotion regulation and adjustment that lends insight into potential developmental processes linking harsh and rejecting parenting with childhood depression. Specifically, and elaborating on the work of Eisenberg and colleagues (1998), Morris and colleagues (2007) posited that children learn from the family context about emotion regulation through (1) observation and modeling of parents' own emotion regulation; (2) specific parenting behaviors that pertain to emotion expression and management; and (3) the family emotional climate. Although these potential mechanisms are interrelated, and distinctions among the mechanisms can at times feel somewhat arbitrary, the model nonetheless provides a useful framework for thinking about the different ways in which family processes may contribute to childhood depression. With respect to the social learning of emotional expression and management, children may learn about emotional management by observing how their parents express and manage emotions in different situations, by looking to their parents for cues about how to respond to different situations (i.e., social referencing) or by mirroring parent affect (i.e., emotion contagion; Dodge, 1993; Silk et al., 2006). Parents may also teach children about emotion display rules and management, such as by encouraging or discouraging specific forms of emotion expression whether explicitly (e.g., emotion coaching) or implicitly (e.g., through reactions to children's expressed emotions), by teaching coping strategies, and by providing children with opportunities to experience and regulate different kinds of emotions (Morelen et al., 2016; Wu et al., 2019).

Research about the ways in which the family emotional climate may influence risk for child depression is most closely aligned with clinical perspectives about family origins of risk and aligns with cognitive-developmental and attachment perspectives from developmental science. These perspectives share a common view in which parent–child interactions are believed to serve as a microcosm through which children develop cognitive schema about the self, others, and the world (Abela & Hankin, 2008; Dodge, 1993). Parenting that is warm, accepting, consistent, and promotes autonomy lays a foundation for children to develop a positive sense of self ("I am deserving of love and warmth") and mastery or agency ("I am capable of shaping my circumstances with the choices I make"). Additionally, when parenting is consistent, children develop a sense of understanding about the world that it is predictable. From an attachment perspective, parent–child relationships and positive marital relationships also form the basis through which children begin to construct schema about the nature and dynamic qualities of interpersonal relationships ("Other people are generally good and loving"; "Others are dependable and trustworthy"). In contrast, parenting that is harsh, rejecting, unpredictable, and undermines autonomy instills a view that others are generally unforgiving and exacting ("Others cannot be trusted"; "Others are always judging me and noticing my flaws") and that the self is often inadequate or undeserving ("I am not good enough"; "There is little I can do to change my circumstance"). Furthermore, because parents who engage in harsh parenting practices tend to minimize or discount children's perspective and to dole out punishments that "don't fit the crime," these practices may over time instill a sense of helplessness and hopelessness about the world as a place that is largely unfair and unreasonable and one they have little agency to change. In turn, these core schema serve as a basis for cognitive vulnerabilities such as those discussed in Section 5.1.4. Indeed, harsh and rejecting parenting has been found to predict a depressogenic attributional style, more self-criticism, and dysfunctional attitudes and cognitive distortions (Abela & Hankin, 2008; Cole et al., 2016).

The consequences of harsh parenting for children's adjustment vary across cultures, socioeconomic groups, and children's sexes (Chen & Liu, 2012; Halgunseth et al., 2006) and are likely shaped in part by cultural attitudes and norms surrounding parenting. Lansford and colleagues (2005) found that the extent to which parents use of corporal punishment, a form of harsh parenting, is associated with children's adjustment depends in part on children's perceptions of the normativeness of and reasons underlying corporal punishment. Furthermore, some evidence supports the notion that parenting practices traditionally construed of as harsh may, in some contexts, better reflect adaptive parenting strategies that fit the demand characteristics of the broader environmental context. For example, drawing data from a sample of Mexican American families, White and colleagues (2019) found that parent perceptions of neighborhood danger were directly associated with mothers' use of harsh parenting practices. Thus, caution should be applied when generalizing associations about the consequences of parenting and its depressogenic implications to socioeconomically and culturally diverse families.

5.3.4 Fathers and the Contributions of Same- or Mixed-Sex Dyadic Structures

Research considering the contributions of parent stress and especially parent depression to child socioemotional development has historically focused on maternal depression. Nevertheless, burgeoning research indicates that paternal depression also contributes to child depression and that it does so over and above maternal depression. Taken in concert with the notion that paternal depression and maternal depression often co-occur in heterosexual family structures (Goodman, 2004; Paulson & Bazemore, 2010), paternal depression likely confers an additive, if not multiplicative, risk for the development of depressive symptoms in childhood. Similar to maternal depression, paternal depression can contribute to developmental risk by undermining the quality of fathering behaviors (Sweeney & MacBeth, 2016; Wilson & Durbin, 2010). In infancy, fathers with depression are less engaged, less responsive, and more withdrawn in interactions with their infants compared to fathers without depression (McElwain & Volling, 1999; Sethna et al., 2018; Sethna et al., 2015). In the toddler years and beyond, paternal depressive symptoms likewise show small but robust associations with more negative (e.g., harsh) and fewer positive (e.g., warmth) parenting behaviors (Wilson & Durbin, 2010) and child poorer socioemotional adjustment (Sweeney & MacBeth, 2016). Beyond the direct effects of paternal depression on infant and child development, scholars have posited that paternal depression may confer risk for child depression and adjustment problems indirectly, such as by influencing levels of maternal depression (Ip et al., 2018) or maternal parenting behaviors (Newland et al., 2015) or by contributing to higher levels of marital conflict (Cummings et al., 2005; Sweeney & MacBeth, 2016).

From a family systems perspective, some evidence suggests that, among heterosexual family structures, fathers' well-being and children's functioning may be somewhat less closely coupled compared to mothers' and children's. For example, paternal depression has been found to exert more indirect influences on children's than maternal depression (Sweeney & MacBeth, 2016). In a study that drew data from the Avon Longitudinal Study of Parents and Children (ALPSAC), a population-based cohort study of families in England, Gutierrez-Galve and colleagues (2015) found that, whereas family factors accounted for two-thirds of the relations between paternal depression and children's adjustment, family factors accounted for less than a quarter of the relations between maternal depression and children's adjustment. Similarly, fathers' parenting engagement and quality may be more likely to deteriorate in the face of family stressors (e.g., maternal depression, marital conflict and dissatisfaction) than is mothers' (Newland et al., 2015; Vallotton et al., 2016; Williams, 2018). Furthermore, fathers' more distal influences appear to be especially pronounced when children are younger, with a preliminary pattern of findings suggestive that links between paternal depression and children's adjustment are less robust in studies of younger versus older children (Connell & Goodman, 2002; Natsuaki et al., 2014). Braungart-Rieker and colleagues (2014) posited that the weaker associations between paternal depression and children's adjustment may reflect differences in maternal versus paternal involvement earlier in childhood and especially during infancy. By extension, it makes sense to think that the greater vulnerability of the father–child relationship to family stressors may also vary as a function of sociocultural expectations about the prominence of father's emotional and behavioral engagement in the family. If so, then these relations will likely differ across cultures, generations, and diverse family structures due to differences in gender role expectations (Braungart-Rieker et al., 2014).

The hypothesis that fathers' contributions to problems such as depressive symptoms may vary as a function of gender role expectations remains to be tested, yet some preliminary evidence suggests that associations may indeed differ among fathers who are highly engaged in routine childcare activities. In a study that drew data from a sample of Mexican American families in which fathers were, on average, nearly as engaged as mothers in routine infant care activities, Lin and colleagues (2020) found that paternal depressive symptoms showed even more robust associations with infant parasympathetic regulatory development than did maternal depressive symptoms. Nevertheless, Lin and colleagues did not formally test whether associations varied as a function of fathers' involvement, and direct tests of this hypotheses are warranted.

Another understudied area of research concerns whether the effects of maternal and paternal depression may differ depending on child, and especially infant, sex. One promising hypothesis in need of investigation is that links between parent depression and infant and child adjustment may vary depending on the same-sex (e.g., mother–daughter, father–son) or mixed-sex (e.g., father–daughter, mother–son) composition of parent–child dyads (Feldman, 2007a; Tronick & Reck, 2009). For example, when considering dyadic interactions in infancy, Feldman (2003) observed that same-sex parent–infant dyads show more synchrony (i.e., higher coherence, mutuality in the lead-lag structure, shorter time-lags to synchrony) in their interactions than mixed-sex parent–infant dyads do. As a result, she posited that mixed-sex parent–infant dyads, which are already inherently less synchronous, may be more vulnerable to additional disruptions via parent depression. Maternal depression has been linked to greater disruptions to mother–son compared to mother–daughter interactions, with both mothers and sons showing more negative affect (Beeghly et al., 2002; Weinberg & Tronick, 1996), more constricted interactions (Sravish et al., 2013), and more difficulty recovering from distress (Weinberg et al., 2006; Weinberg & Tronick, 1996). Taken together, father depression may show differential associations with depressive experience in young children depending on the extent of father involvement in routine caregiving inter-actions, sociocultural and generational factors that shape family and parent–infant interaction dynamics, and infant sex. Nevertheless, given the paucity of literature that addresses the contributions of father depression to parent–infant interactions or sex differences, it remains to be seen whether these patterns stand up to replication and, if so, whether they generalize across diverse family structures.

5.4 Peer Processes

Whereas the family represents the foremost context in which children are embedded early in life, the peer context comprises an increasingly salient developmental context from the school-age years onward. In parallel to risk factors that have emerged in the family, peer rejection and victimization repre-sent the most prominent risk contributors to childhood depression (Gardner et al., 2009; Reijntjes et al., 2010). For example, in a study that followed more than 400 children from second (approximately 7–9 years old) to fifth grade (10–12 years old), Rudolph and colleagues (2011) found that both initial levels of peer victimization (i.e., in second grade) and increases in peer victimization over time were uniquely associated with increases in depressive symptoms in fifth grade. Furthermore, the associations between peer victimization and depression are likely bidirectional, such that children who show increases in depression are also more likely to become victimized over time (Bilsky et al.,

2013; Mlawer et al., 2019; Reijntjes et al., 2010). Peer victimization can occur in person or through online formats (i.e., cyberbullying). However, because there is substantial overlap between traditional forms of bullying and cyberbullying, it is difficult to delineate whether there are unique consequences associated with cyberbullying (Olweus & Limber, 2018).

The mechanisms that link peer rejection and victimization to childhood depression are not well understood. However, similar to harsh and rejecting parenting, peer rejection and victimization are believed to contribute to the development of maladaptive cognitions about the self and others (Crick & Ladd, 1993; Haines et al., 1999), all of which may in turn further exacerbate social difficulties. A limited number of studies to date tested these hypotheses in samples of children, yet they have yielded supportive evidence that peer rejection and victimization may engender maladaptive cognitions including depressive attributional styles (Bilsky et al., 2013; Gibb & Abela, 2008), negative self-concept (Cole et al., 2014), and lower self-perceptions of social competence (Bilsky et al., 2013; Cole et al., 1997). Some evidence further suggests that the influence of peer victimization on these emerging cognitions may be more domain-specific than the influence of harsh parenting. In a cross-sequential study of third (8–10-year-olds) and sixth graders (11–13-year-olds), Cole and colleagues (1997) found that, whereas harsh parenting was associated with higher general negative cognitive attributions and lower general positive cognitive attributions, peer victimization showed narrowband associations with poorer social and interpersonal cognitions (e.g., low interpersonal efficacy and competence). Scholars have theorized that repeated experiences of peer victimization may undermine attempts to cope and ultimately to cultivate feelings of helplessness. In a prospective longitudinal study that followed children from third (8–10 years) to sixth grade (11–13 years), Troop-Gordon and colleagues (2015) found that peer victimization preceded decreased engagement coping and increased avoidant coping.

Perhaps unsurprisingly by this point, it seems important to reiterate that several of the child risk characteristics discussed likely transact with peer factors to influence the incidence of both child rejection and victimization and subsequent depression. For example, some evidence suggests that child perceptions of rejection may be an even more salient prediction of depressive symptoms than actual experiences of rejection (Kistner et al., 1999). In a study that followed fourth and fifth graders (9–12-year-olds) over the course of seven years, Kistner and colleagues (1999) found that, whereas children's perceptions of peer acceptance was associated with subsequent dysphoria, actual acceptance (i.e., as measured using peer sociometric ratings of children's acceptance) was not. Thus, initial cognitive vulnerabilities or related dispositional proclivities for negative emotionality may also prompt a self-perpetuating cycle of peer rejection and depression (Garber & Rao, 2014; Rudolph et al., 2009).

5.5 Contextual Stressors

The relevance of children's broader environmental context has long been recognized, with seminal theories of development emphasizing the relevance of both proximal and distal factors for shaping children's development (e.g., bioecological theory; integrative model for the study of developmental competencies in minority children; Bronfenbrenner & Morris, 2007; Garcia Coll et al., 1996). Considered with respect to childhood depression, contextual stressors such as SES, poverty, neighborhood disadvantage, and exposure to racism and discrimination may comprise discrete stressors themselves and may compound risk by increasing the likelihood of multiple stress exposure. For example, and as we alluded to in our earlier discussion of the dependency of stressors, the integrative model for the study of developmental competencies in minority children (Garcia Coll et al., 1996) has underscored the importance of considering how an individual's social position within a given society may also influence the number and severity of neighborhood, family, and peer stressors a child may face (Figure 3).

Consistent with this suggestion, low SES has been found to predict early-onset depression (Hastings et al., 2015; Leech et al., 2006). Furthermore, evidence suggests that associations between low SES and child depression may be mediated by the indirect effects of SES on more proximal risk factors such as temperament (Hopkins et al., 2013), cognitive vulnerability (Culpin et al., 2015), and family stress (Conger et al., 2002; Hopkins et al., 2013). Additionally, disparities in childhood SES and exposure to stressful life events have been found to account for disparities in depressive symptoms among African Americans and Latin Americans compared to European Americans (Adkins et al., 2009).

Compared to the vast literature investigating the consequences of socioeconomic and financial strain, considerably less research has been devoted to clarifying the extent to which other stressors secondary to social position, such as interpersonal discrimination and structural racism, may likewise contribute to childhood depression. In a meta-analysis, Priest and colleagues (2013) found that the effects of interpersonal discrimination on adjustment were most pronounced when considering child outcomes at birth (e.g., birth weight, which may signal psychobiological risk for depression) as well as among primary and high school students (e.g., physical and mental health). In contrast, the effects of

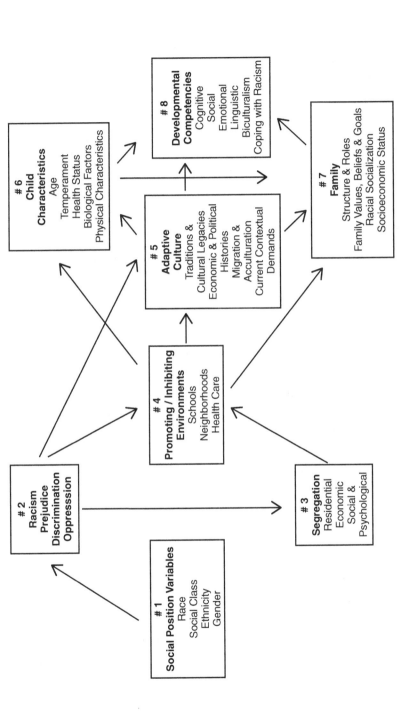

Figure 3 Integrative model for the study of developmental competencies in minority children

Note: From "An Integrative Model for the Study of Developmental Competencies in Minority Children," by C. Garcia Coll, G. Lamberty, R. Jenkins, H. Pipes McAdoo, K. A. Crnic, B. H. Wasik, H. Vasquez Garcia, Child Development, 67, p. 1896.

interpersonal discrimination on adjustment were weakest among preschool-age children. Several potential mediators also emerged, most of which align with the risk factors for depression in children discussed in Section 5 thus far, including ethnic self-identity and esteem, perceived stress, and intergroup competence in interactions with peers.

Systematic oppression, as in the form of structural racism, is difficult to measure. Nevertheless, some methods that may prove promising may include the quantification of neighborhood-level characteristics, such as neighborhood quality and violence, ethnic segregation, median neighborhood income, and proximity to environmental toxicants; time- or geographically based comparisons of the impacts of discriminatory policies; or other similar, population-based metrics. For example, Acevedo-Garcia and colleagues (2014) developed a compelling Child Opportunity Index (COI), a multidimensional index that quantifies neighborhood-level features, including access to a range of educational, health and environmental, and social and economic opportunities, within a given census tract. In another example, Stephens-Davidowitz (2014) utilized "big data" obtained from Google search queries of racially charged language to develop a proxy variable for levels of racial animus in various geographic regions in the United States. These and other creative methods that draw from interdisciplinary insights and leverage technological advances to quantify constructs that have historically been more difficult to capture may prove critical in the next generation of research examining contextual influences on the development of competencies and the occurrence of mental health risks such as childhood depression.

Few studies to date have investigated the downstream consequences of structural oppression on childhood depression; emergent studies yield support for the notion that it likewise has noxious implications for children's development and well-being. For example, nascent research suggests that indices of systemic racism may undergird infant poorer birth outcomes (Chae et al., 2018; Wallace, 2011), which can cascade into a variety of mental health concerns including depression. Greater integration of indices of systemic racism and discrimination into research considering the developmental processes through which contextual stressors may influence health and well-being among vulnerable populations may help to clarify the social determinants of physical and mental health disparities. Additionally, attention to the ways in which systemic forms of oppression may benefit members of privileged groups may be equally important for clarifying these effects (Seaton et al., 2018). Finally, equally important as research considering risk processes, research considering unique individual, familial, cultural, and community resilience processes that buffer against the noxious effects of marginalization will be critical for clarifying culturally responsive ways in which to offset their effects.

Importantly, the consequences of interpersonal and structural racism and discrimination likely vary both within and across nations and may wax and wane in salience with current events and the ever-changing sociopolitical landscape. For example, the currently ongoing Covid-19 pandemic has had an outsized effect on children, parents, and families (Bornstein, 2021), with substantial increases observed in reports of child and parent depression (Nearchou et al., 2020). Furthermore, burgeoning research indicates that the social and emotional impact of the Covid-19 pandemic on children and parents is likely particularly pronounced among racial and ethnic minority families (Benner & Mistry, 2020). Additionally, a growing body of research evaluating the impact of digital media and technology use – both of which are also elevated among low SES families – may undermine parent sensitivity and engagement in ways that are consequential for child emotional development (McDaniel & Radesky, 2018). In fact, one study by Stockdale and colleagues (2020) found that infants exhibited similar distress behaviors during a parent phone-distracted task (i.e., "technoference") as they did in response to the still-face paradigm (i.e., simulations of parent depressed affect). Greater integration of these considerations may help to clarify the ways in which contextual stressors underlie the developmental origins of mental health disparities, especially including depression, among children from marginalized communities.

6 Developmental Consequences of Depression in Children's Lives

Whether depression presents as subclinical or as disorder, and whether it is experienced directly in the child or as through experience with a depressed parent, depressive experience has developmental consequences. These consequences run the gamut from comorbidities with related behavior and emotional problems, to cognitive and academic impairments, to social skill and peer relationship difficulties, to family distress. Some research suggests that consequences tend to be more severe when depressive disorder is present and recurrent as opposed to the presence of symptom or syndrome only (Avenevoli et al., 2008) but subclinical depression has also been found to be associated with greater levels of impairment across developmental domains (Wesselhoeft et al., 2016).

6.1 Consequences of Childhood Depression

As with any atypical condition of childhood, the potential consequences of depressive experience and disorder are of substantial concern. Although resilience processes operate to produce multifinal outcomes (Fergusson & Horwood, 2003), there are a number of developmental domains at risk in young children.

6.1.1 Behavior and Emotion Problems

As emotionally and behaviorally challenging as depression is for those children who experience it, rarely does the condition occur in isolation. Children with elevated depressive symptoms or depressive disorder often have one or more other disorders or sets of symptoms that coexist with these depressive features. In fact, Garber and Rao (2014) reported that comorbidities are found in 42 percent of depressed children in community samples and in more than 75 percent of clinical identified samples. Among the common comorbidities are anxiety disorders (especially separation anxiety disorder), conduct disorder, and attention deficit hyperactivity disorder (Harrington et al., 2000; Yorbik et al., 2004). Wolff and Ollendick (2006) reported a reciprocal relation between depression and aggression, following reports by Lahey and colleagues (2002) that there is a dynamic relation between depression and conduct disorder such that, when depression increases over time, a tendency exists for it to be followed by like increases in conduct problems. Furthermore, the comorbidity between depression and conduct problems tends to vary with both child age and sex (Wagner, 2003), such that both depression and conduct problems tend to increase with age, and the comorbidity of these two problems tends to occur more in boys than girls.

A fair amount of work has also specifically addressed the co-occurrence of anxiety with depression during childhood. This may be the most common comorbidity found for children with depressive symptoms, which is not surprising in that both depression and anxiety are aspects of negative affectivity even though their phenomenology can be quite different. In their systematic review of comorbid anxiety and depression in children and adolescents, Melton and colleagues (2016) reported that, when anxiety and depression occur together, the symptoms are typically more severe, a more chronic course of the disorder is likely, and increased somatic complaints are involved. Furthermore, subthreshold depressive symptoms show greater likelihood of becoming later full disorder when anxiety co-occurs, albeit more often for girls than boys. The growing attention to subsyndromal levels of the disorders reflects the more current emphasis on dimensional perspectives, and DSM-5 acknowledges this perspective with an added specifier within the depression category that describes a condition of depression with anxious distress. This condition requires an major depressive disorder (MDD) diagnosis and at least two anxious symptoms (e.g., feeling tense, unusually restless) that are also present during the depression episode. The important question is whether early depressive symptoms, either subclinical or at the level of disorder, give rise to later anxiety. Although there is some evidence to suggest that such directions of effect exist, the most well-designed studies find stronger evidence in support of anxiety predictions to depression in childhood and adolescence (Cole et al., 1998; Melton et al., 2016). Regardless, the presence of depressive disorder or symptoms during childhood, including lower social competence in general, conveys risk for the experience of related behavioral and emotional problems.

6.1.2 Cognitive and Academic Functioning

Considering the symptom complex associated with childhood depression, it is unsurprising to find that children who present with depressive symptoms are at risk for general cognitive delays, specific cognitive deficits, and ongoing academic impairment. Low motivation, inattentiveness, lethargy, and lack of concentration are all likely attributes that adversely affect cognitive function and learning. Early explorations of the connections between depression and cognitive or academic skills showed these expected adverse associations (Fauber et al., 1987), although measurement and methodological issues clouded the connections observed (McGee & Williams, 1988). Childhood depressive symptoms have been reported to be associated with later academic impairment, although the effects appear to be more severe when conduct problems co-occur with depression (Ingoldsby et al., 2006).

Although findings in support of academic impairment are generally robust, the connections between depression and cognitive competence are both complex and controversial as the findings in support of such connections are generally weak and the direction of effect has sometimes been debated. Some evidence has emerged to support the connection between childhood depression and later cognitive impairment both in global cognitive ability (Beaujean et al., 2013) and for discrete cognitive abilities involving executive functions (EF) such as sustained attention (Brooks et al., 2010), response inhibition (Cataldo et al., 2005), and set shifting (Emerson et al., 2005), among others. However, quite a few other studies that have attempted to find these same EF deficits in depressed children could not (Vilgis et al., 2015). In fact, Vilgis and colleagues noted that, in their review of thirty-three studies of children with diagnosed depressive disorders, there was a greater tendency toward null results than support for a meaningful association between depression and EF abilities. With respect to alternative directions of effect, Bornstein and colleagues (2013) demonstrated across both early and later childhood samples that early language skill deficits were associated with the emergence of internalizing problems later. Clearly, although findings may be suggestive of connections, the issue of whether childhood depression is associated with EF and other cognitive deficits is not yet resolved and awaits further research.

6.1.3 Peer Relationships and Social Skills

A substantial amount of attention has been paid to the ways in which childhood depression may impact children's social skills development and peer relationships across childhood. We touched on this issue in Section 5 on etiologies of childhood depression but address it again here with a more specific focus on the consequences of child depression for peer and social adjustment. Overall, research indicates that risk is apparent as childhood depression is associated with multiple social skill deficits, poorer quality friendships, victimization, and greater levels of peer rejection (Prinstein et al., 2005; Rudolph et al., 2008).

It has been suggested that depressed children develop distorted perceptions of their social relationships wherein depressed children see themselves as being less socially competent and as experiencing greater levels of peer rejection (Brendgen et al., 2002). Such distorted perceptions of social relationships occur in concert with behaviors that create negative reactions from peers and generate more stressors for depressed children (Rudolph et al., 2008). Indeed, Rudolph (2009) described a self-perpetuating cycle in which the depressed child's perception of peer rejection leads to either withdrawal from peers or hostility toward them. In turn, that withdrawal or hostility results in some level of negative reaction from peers, and these negative reactions then serve to reinforce the depressed child's perception of rejection, perpetuating the peer rejection cycle and promoting maintenance of depressive conditions.

Bullying and peer victimization have been a focus of substantial attention in depressed children. It seems apparent that the presence of depressive symptoms undermines children's status over time (Kochel et al., 2012), and a focus on the symptom level of child depression has yielded especially rich findings. Depressive symptoms have been linked to peer victimization as well as peer rejection (Choukas-Bradley & Prinstein, 2014) and most strongly so in late childhood and during times of school transition (Krygsman & Vaillancourt, 2017). Krygsman and Vaillancourt also noted that the source of the reports for these findings is important, as peer victimization was predominantly tied to child self-reports whereas meaningful associations between depressed symptoms and peer rejection were apparent across reporters. This finding suggests that child report is a critical methodological need, as constructs such as victimization may predominantly occur outside of the attention of responsible adults.

Agoston and Rudolph (2013) examined pathways to explain associations between depressive symptoms and peer neglect and peer rejection in children at two age periods. Across middle childhood (mean age 7.9 years) as well as late childhood/early adolescence (mean age 11.7 years), they explored the pathways through which social helplessness in middle childhood, and aggression in late childhood, might be tied to relations between depressive symptoms and peer neglect and rejection. Assessing each of the factors across three waves during the school year, they found the presence of complex pathways of influence for each age period. For the younger children, depressive symptoms at Wave 1 were associated with greater social helplessness at Wave 2, and social helplessness in turn predicted more peer neglect and rejection at Wave 3. Furthermore, social helplessness mediated relations between depression and peer neglect and rejection in middle childhood. In later childhood, more reported depressive symptoms predicted more aggressiveness, which in turn predicted more peer rejection but not neglect. Aggression mediated relations between depression and peer rejection but not neglect likely because aggression is much more difficult to ignore than are behaviors associated with social helplessness.

In summary, research supports pathways from childhood depressive experience to peer problems and social competence concerns, identifying conditions that place depressed children at risk for social neglect, rejection, and victimization depending on various social-cognitive and behavioral issues. The cyclical nature of these peer and social problems may play an important role in the continuity of childhood depression over time and into adolescence.

6.2 Consequences of Parental Depression

In Section 5.3, we addressed issues involved with parental depression as a determinant or risk factor for the emergence of childhood depression. In this section, we discuss the broader developmental consequences of parental depression, and the mechanisms involved, touching specifically on the consequences for parenting itself as well as its ramifications for children's emotional well-being, emotion regulation, broader adjustment concerns, and cognitive and academic impairments.

Goodman has provided the most extensive compilation of work addressing parental depression and its developmental consequences for children and families. Across a number of reviews (Goodman & Gotlib, 1999; Goodman et al., 2011; Goodman, 2020; Goodman et al., 2020) as well as many individual studies that address various aspects of the developmental model of understanding mechanisms of transmission (Goodman & Gotlib, 1999), Goodman and colleagues explicated the complexity of connections between parental depression and children's development as well as identified a variety of mechanisms that likely underlie such connections. Among the operative mechanisms, Goodman proposed that genetic factors, dysfunctional neuroregulatory mechanisms, and exposure to the mother's maladaptive affect, behavior, and cognitions operate in concert over time to create the increased risk for children across developmental domains. Contextual stressors frequently associated with maternal depression contribute critically as well. While touching on a number of modifiers that might exacerbate the connections between maternal depression and adverse child outcomes, she also noted that nonadaptive outcomes are not ubiquitous and suggested the need to better understand modifiers that also reduce intergenerational transmission and risk.

6.2.1 Parenting Behavior and Attitudes

One of the primary risks of maternal depression is its adverse effect on parenting behavior and attitudes. This is important not only in that depression often directly affects the ways that parents behave with and think about their children but also because parenting behavior is frequently conceptualized as a key pathway through which maternal depression links to a variety of child development and adjustment attributes. Indeed, changes in parental behavior consequent to depressive episodes or symptom increases are often considered to be one primary mechanism through which parental depression exerts its influence on children's functioning.

Parental depression, most often maternal, has been associated with a wide variety of parenting behaviors, most of which would be considered problematic to support positive child development. Lovejoy and colleagues (2000) conducted a meta-analysis of forty-six studies of observed parenting behavior in mothers who were identified as depressed, grouping observed parenting constructs into three factors involving negative/hostile, disengaged, or positive social behavior. They found moderate effect sizes for maternal depression as well as both increased negative hostile and disengaged parenting behavior and small effect sizes for the association between maternal depression and less positive parenting behaviors. A number of moderators influenced the nature of the associations that were found. Among them, connections between maternal depression and parenting were stronger for current depressive status as opposed to lifetime depression status, and the effects of depression on parenting were most pronounced for infants and young children. One caveat was that it was not certain that the effects were always depression-specific as opposed to being a function of more general distress in the mother.

Multiple studies since have likewise found that parenting behavior may be compromised in mothers who are depressed. In a longitudinal study of first-time mothers, Norcross and colleagues (2020) found that mothers who reported higher levels of depressive symptoms were less sensitive to infant distress, a link that was exacerbated in families with greater SES risk. In a study of mothers of preschoolers, Hoffman and colleagues (2006) found that mothers who reported higher depressive symptoms were less effective scaffolders of their children's problem-solving. Others have found that depressed parents show reduced positive expression over time (Feng et al., 2007) and used more physical discipline and harsh, critical parenting (Murray et al., 2010). Similarly, low reciprocity and low engagement (Feldman, 2007b) have been tied to maternal depression. Using UK Millennium Study data, Kiernan and Huerta (2008) found that mothers who are depressed use harsher disciplinary practices, have a less positive relationship with their children, and spend somewhat less time on reading activities. In another large database study (Fragile Families and Child Well-Being study), Turney (2012) found some support for less engagement longitudinally, but causal connections between depressed parents and problematic parenting over time for other parenting behaviors could not be clearly established. Azaka and Raeder (2013) assessed trajectories of parenting behaviors across infancy and toddler periods and found that mothers who showed comorbid anxiety and depression showed the most problematic parenting styles, but their parenting quality increased over time despite elevated depression scores. Although most of these studies address maternal depression in particular, Wilson and Durbin (2010) found similar relations for depressed fathers and parenting behaviors in their meta-analytic study of paternal depression and parenting.

Clearly, parental depression has some influence on the nature of parenting that children receive, and these influences may vary as a function of the age of the children, the SES status of the family, marital or family status, ongoing familial stressors, and an array of other moderators that operate to influence the links between parental depression and parenting processes (Taraban et al., 2017). Although parenting is clearly at risk in the context of depression, whether it serves to mediate the critical connection between parent depression and child development is a key conceptual issue in understanding depression in children's lives. We address that issue further in the sections that follow.

6.2.2 Behavioral and Emotional Adjustment

The effects of parental depression on children's behavioral and emotional well-being have been a topic of great interest, especially in understanding whether the connection may be direct or indirect. We address those issues here, omitting consideration of childhood depression as an outcome as that has been addressed in Section 5.3.

There is overwhelming support for links between parental depressive symptoms and children's behavioral and emotional adjustment. Across studies and across child ages, investigators find evidence that maternal and paternal depression, in either symptom or disorder form, is associated with more problematic functioning in offspring (Campbell et al., 2009; Cheung & Theule, 2019; Kane & Garber, 2004; Van der Waerden et al., 2015). Goodman and colleagues (2011) reported less positive affect and more negative affect, as well as higher internalizing and externalizing behavior problems overall, in children of depressed mothers. A metanalysis of the connection between parental depression and child negativity found that parental prenatal and postnatal depression were positively linked with child negative affect, although prenatal connections were stronger for mothers than fathers (Spry et al., 2020). In studies assessing more specific behavioral and emotional attributes, Hoffman and colleagues (2006) found that higher maternal depressive symptoms at age three predicted lower child emotion regulation abilities at age four, while Gartstein and Fagot (2003) described negative associations between maternal depressive symptoms and young children's effortful control. Manian and Bornstein (2009), using a still-face paradigm, demonstrated that infants of clinically depressed mothers used more internally directed self-soothing strategies whereas infants of nondepressed mothers used more attention regulation strategies to reduce negativity. DeRose and colleagues (2014) reported connections between persistent maternal depression and social skills in ten-to-eleven-year-olds, while in a longitudinal investigation spanning ten years Priel and colleagues (2020) found that, by age ten, children who had been exposed to maternal depression showed emotion recognition deficits as well as less social collaboration in observed interactions with the parent.

Mothers have been the focus of the greatest amount of research on connections between parental depression and child development, but fathers have also been the focus of study. Cummings and colleagues explored the links between paternal depression and children's adjustment across a number of studies, detailing not only pathways that show relations between paternal depression and emotional insecurity (Cummings et al., 2013) but also that depression in fathers, in the context of the marital relationship, has implications for children's behavioral adjustment that extend above and beyond those of mothers (Cummings et al., 2010). Also supporting the importance of father–child processes, Jacob and Johnson (1997) found that, although mother and father depression status was similar in accounting for child behavior problems, father–child communication moderated the associations while maternal–child communication did not, suggesting an especially important role for father–child interaction in the transmission process.

In summary, there is ample evidence that both parental depressive symptoms and depressive disorder are correlates of child behavior and emotion problems above and beyond those specific to emerging child depression. This appears to be true whether the depression is present in mothers or fathers. Although the effects appear to be more potent at younger child ages, they are apparent across childhood. Yet the pathways through which parental depression connects to child well-being are neither always simple nor always direct. Rather, explanatory mechanisms involve complex pathways of influence that depend on parenting processes to bridge the connection between parental depression and child adjustment. Even so, the exploration of mediation and moderation processes is not always fruitful in providing evidence in support of parenting as the connector between parent depression and child developmental outcome. For example, Hoffman and colleagues (2006) failed to find evidence that maternal scaffolding mediated the relation between maternal depressive symptoms and observed emotion regulation quality in preschool-age children. Still, parent-mediated processes are one frequent explanation for understanding the ways that depression in the parent might affect the developmental well-being of the child, and there is supportive evidence for this mechanism involving elements of parent stress as well as parenting behavior (Baker & Kuhn, 2018; DeRose et al., 2014; Fredriksen et al., 2019; Kuckertz et al., 2018; Wang & Dix, 2017). Regarding evidence in support of parenting mediation, Goodman (2020) has also described the importance of child vulnerabilities as mediators of linkages that are typically found between parent depression and child well-being. Goodman suggests that there are likely multiple mediators operative at any one developmental point in time (see also Baker & Kuhn, 2018; Priel et al., 2019), and a recent meta-analysis of studies exploring parenting processes as mediators of the connection between parental depression and child well-being found a small but significant effect for parenting as one mechanism (Goodman et al., 2020). Nevertheless, there remains much to be explored in determining the complex nature of the multiply mediated and moderated pathways involved.

6.2.3 Cognitive and Academic Impairment

Although the lion's share of the research on the effect of parent depressive symptoms on offspring has addressed the effects on parenting behavior and children's behavioral and emotional adjustment, a sizeable literature has also emerged on the development of cognitive ability and academic functioning. Similar to the research in other functional domains, parental depression appears to convey meaningful risks for cognitive and academic impairment.

Considering the emotional and behavioral decrements associated with parental depression, it was perhaps logical to surmise that there could also be risk to children's global cognitive functioning. Many studies have assessed relations between maternal depression and child IQ or developmental functioning, and the evidence does not entirely converge toward a single clear picture. A preponderance of the work, however, seems to suggest that there are small effects demonstrating risk for global cognitive deficit (Stein ct al., 2014), and the effects may be related to depression chronicity (Cornish et al., 2005). Still, some studies failed to find expected associations (Murray et al., 1996; Piteo et al., 2012; Tse et al., 2010). There is some evidence from longitudinal studies to suggest that concurrent levels of depression may have more predictive weight than assessments from earlier periods in the prediction to general cognitive ability (Sutter-Dallay et al., 2011), a finding that supports arguments against sensitive period conceptualizations (Evans et al., 2012). Greater chronicity of depression also seems to be an important determinant of whether an adverse effect on cognition emerges.

In contrast to the more equivocal findings on general cognitive ability, research offers somewhat stronger support for associations between parental depression and children's EF (Snyder, 2013). In a study assessing the connection of parent perinatal depression to poor academic achievement in adolescents, Pearson and colleagues (2016) found that attentional control at age eight connected early perinatal depression and academic functioning in adolescence, although this finding emerged only for mothers' perinatal depression status, not fathers'. In their longitudinal study, Hughes and colleagues (2013) found that both mean levels and chronicity of maternal depression were significantly associated with child EF at age six, with lower average levels and steeper declines in depression associated with better child EF at age six. Mean level of maternal depression was important for some skills such as working memory, whereas inhibitory control was more affected by change in depression. In another longitudinal study, Wang and Dix (2017) found that maternal depressive symptoms during infancy, independent of later depression, uniquely predicted poor sustained attention and EF in children at school entry. While these findings are compelling, several other studies failed to find associations between parental depression and children's EF skills (Rhoades et al., 2011; Micco et al., 2009; Vilgis et al., 2015). Sample size (power) and sample characteristic differences, including child age and ethnicity, may help to explain the differences in findings to some extent.

Several studies have examined other early cognitive skills and the connection to maternal depression, again showing that exposure to depression is associated with decrements in cognitive function for young children. With clinically depressed mothers, infants demonstrated poorer object processing skills (Bornstein et al., 2012) and likewise had more difficulty discriminating a neutral face from a smiling one (Bornstein et al., 2011). Language skills have also shown decrements with maternal depression (Bornstein et al., in press), although these have also been associated specifically with fathers' depression (Fredriksen et al., 2019).

In Section 6.1.2, we noted that academic impairment is found in children who present with depressive symptoms. Similar results emerge when the depression context is familial or parental (Goodman, 2020). Augustine and Crosnoe (2010) found connections between maternal depression and children's academic achievement only when mothers had a high school education or below but not when mothers were more highly educated. Wang and Dix (2017) found that postpartum depression was associated with children's cognitive adjustment in third grade, with this relation mediated by child EF skills. Wright and colleagues (2000) also found that teachers reported more academic problems for eight-year-old children whose mothers reported more depressive symptoms between child ages three months to three years. Although the evidence is not especially compelling overall, there does seem to be some degree of support for the notion that children of depressed parents, again typically mothers, present with academic impairments. It seems likely, however, that there is again a wide range of moderators to act to create the multifinality that is frequently seen.

7 Interventions for Depression in Children's Lives

Given the extensive risks that are apparent for children who experience depression in their lives, the need for effective preventive interventions and individual treatments is great. Thankfully, there has been substantial research interest in the development of preventive interventions for such, and several therapies for children with depressive disorder have also been shown to be efficacious and effective. Many impressive efforts have also been directed toward developing preventive interventions that focus on addressing parental depression and its consequences.

7.1 Depression in the Child

A variety of treatments for children who are depressed have produced positive, and in some cases sustainable, effects, although some scholars question the extent to which there is actual empirical support of treatment effectiveness. The most often employed interventions include pharmacological ones that utilize antidepressants, psychological interventions that predominantly involve cognitive behavioral or interpersonal therapies, and treatment approaches that in some cases combine both pharmacological and psychological approaches.

The use of antidepressant medication for children has been controversial, and there is some question about whether or not the equivocal evidence for its effectiveness and possible increased risk for suicidal ideation justifies its use in preadolescents (Cipriani et al., 2016). Nevertheless, antidepressant prescription for children with MDD is increasing internationally (Bachmann et al., 2016), and evidence from meta-analyses suggests that one antidepressant medication (fluoxetine) may have at least modest to medium-sized positive effects on MDD in children and minimal risk for increased suicidal ideation (Bridge et al., 2007; Cipriani et al., 2016). Close monitoring of children's response to antidepressant medication is always recommended, and the use of medication as a treatment approach is only warranted by disorder diagnosis.

Psychological interventions that focus on cognitive behavioral (CBT) and interpersonal therapy (IPT) approaches are generally less controversial and can be engaged at the symptom, syndrome, or disorder level of functioning. A number of these treatment approaches have been reported to be efficacious in ameliorating depressive conditions in children across a variety of individual studies and several conceptual reviews or meta-analyses (e.g., Bose & Pettit, 2018; Crowe & McKay, 2017; David-Ferdon & Kaslow, 2008). A more stringently selective recent meta-analytic study suggests, however, that these approaches with depressed children seem to be less successful than they are with depressed adolescents (Weersing et al., 2017). Nevertheless, CBT approaches, especially those that are group-based, are the most effective psychological treatment approaches found with children experiencing depression. It also appears that psychological approaches may be successful with depressed children as young as preschool ages, as Luby and colleagues (2018) demonstrated that a parent–child interaction (PCIT) intervention combined with an emotion development component showed reduced depression diagnoses, reduced symptom severity, less general impairment, and better emotion regulation in the group of children receiving the intervention.

The successful Luby and colleagues (2018) intervention speaks to the importance of family or parent inclusion in the treatment process for children with depressive disorders. Children, and especially young children, are embedded within a family system and depend on parents for nurturance and emotional learning, and therefore parent inclusion is likely to enhance therapeutic effectiveness. The importance of family-focused intervention for children with depression was also demonstrated by Tompson and colleagues (2017) in a study in which posttreatment reductions in depression and increases in social adjustment were found for children aged seven to fourteen years. Dietz and colleagues (2015) likewise showed that a family-based interpersonal therapy treatment, in comparison to a nondirective child-centered intervention, more successfully reduced depression rates, lowered depressive symptoms, and reduced social impairments in depressed children aged seven to twelve. In all, the research suggests that treatment and interventions for children with diagnosed depressive conditions or subclinical symptoms can be successful, especially when the interventions rely on evidence-based practices and include a family focus.

Although the ability of interventions to ameliorate childhood depression to a meaningful degree is certainly welcome, efforts to prevent childhood depression altogether offer even greater potential to positively influence children's well-being. Much is known about the salient risks for depression during the childhood period (see Section 6) that could be the focus of either targeted or universal prevention efforts, but to date most of the prevention efforts have focused on addressing the cognitive and interpersonal facets that facilitate or interfere with emerging emotional competencies. Most of the controlled studies to date were reviewed in Werner-Seidler and colleagues' (2017) meta-analytic review, and the evidence suggests that CBT- and IPT-based prevention programs produce modest but significant short-term benefits for children, with the greatest effects apparent for prevention efforts targeted at children with multiple risks.

7.2 Depression in the Parent

Given that depression in parents has numerous adverse implications for children's development and well-being, many preventive intervention programs focus on ameliorating parent depression. The underlying assumption is that, if parental depression can be reduced or minimized, then the child and family are spared the consequent challenges and risks that are attendant to that condition. This assumption has received some support (Wickramaratne et al., 2011), but treating parent depression alone may not always have the broad familial advantages sought (Gunlicks & Weissman, 2008).

Numerous intervention programs have been directed at reducing parent depression, especially maternal depression occurring during the prenatal and the early postnatal periods. Goodman and Garber (2017) provided a thoughtful discussion of the conceptual and empirical issues involved in research on the treatment of depressed mothers and also reviewed the evidence in support of several home visiting interventions with components that are meant to more specifically target maternal depression. They also reviewed evidence in support of the Triple P parenting program for depressed mothers of preschoolers, indicating that an enhanced Triple P intervention is successful not only in reducing parental depression but in improving parenting practices and reducing children's behavioral adjustment problems. These benefits accrue not only immediately posttreatment but also in extended follow-up. Goodman and Garber (2017) suggested that integrating treatment components that focus on both parental mood states and parenting skills is especially needed, but interventions also need to include more personalized approaches to individual parent needs and then make explicit plans to maintain intervention improvements over time. Drury and colleagues (2016) also reviewed interventions for maternal postpartum depression and suggested that results have been equivocal in the effectiveness of some programs but are better for those programs of individual and dyadic intervention that include facets to improve mother–infant interaction. Still, they caution that long-term follow-up remains a need to support confidence in program success for parent well-being and child development.

Several contemporary interventions for maternal depression have pursued mindfulness training approaches. The evidence suggests that mindfulness interventions can be successful in reducing or preventing depression during the prenatal period (Dhillon et al., 2017) and for the postpartum period as well (Guo et al., 2020; Shulman et al., 2018). Web-based intervention models have also found some success (Lee et al., 2016), especially in that they obviate many of the obstacles that parents find to avoid participating in in-person intervention programs. The Mamma Mia program (Haga et al., 2019), developed in Norway, provides automated web-based information to mothers from prenatal periods to infant age six months, covering a range of risk and protective factors for maternal depression. Results suggest it is effective in producing reductions in postpartum depression at posttreatment and follow-up periods. Likewise, the Be-a-Mom program (Fonseca et al., 2020) is a self-guided web-based intervention that incorporates basic CBT approaches to help mothers address postpartum depression symptoms. Initial analyses provide some evidence for the program's effectiveness in preventing postpartum depression, but it was less effective in addressing related factors such as negative thoughts or marital satisfaction.

In summary, there is substantial evidence in support of interventions for depressed parents to effect important developmental advantages for children of these parents. Preventing or reducing parental depression has advantages not only for the parent's own sense of well-being but also in minimizing child exposure to dysregulated emotion and the developmental consequences that such exposure brings for issues specific to the intergenerational transmission of depression and the consequences for child adjustment more generally.

8 Conclusions

From conceptual, empirical, and practical perspectives, depression in children's lives represents a significant developmental concern. Thankfully, diagnosed depressive disorder is rare during the childhood period, although even rates of

3 percent for "lifetime" prevalence during childhood would suggest that many millions of children are affected. Such numbers are higher than anyone would hope to see. Subclinical depressive experience involving less severe and less frequent symptom expression is more common than clinical disorder, but despite its seemingly normative developmental range, it can carry developmental consequences that are sometimes indistinguishable from those associated with disorder. It would be challenging enough if clinical and subclinical experiences were the only considerations to be addressed in understanding depression in children's lives, but exposure to parental depression and its subsequent effects on parenting processes add another high-risk dimension to children's experience of depression. The context of parental depression presents risk not only for the transmission of depressive experience across generations but to multiple aspects of children's emotional, social, and cognitive competence.

Certainly, theory and research have evolved over the past several decades to expand developmental models of children's experience of depression and the methods used to explore the complex mechanisms that underlie the biological, psychological, and ecological factors at play. Developmental psychopathology perspectives (Cicchetti, 2006; Cicchetti & Toth, 1998) have provided a primary emphasis for this evolution, promoting sophisticated integrative approaches that merge ontogenetic biological and social processes with organizational and transactional perspectives to promote the understanding that there are diverse pathways to disorder as well as competence. Throughout this Element, we have attempted to detail a number of these perspectives and the research that supports models of child and parental depressive experiences that influence the processes by which development unfolds for the child.

Research supports the notion that depressive experience in children can emerge early, and, when it does, the chances for recurrence during childhood increase, perhaps to as much as 60 percent. Although that degree of recurrence is alarming overall, its converse suggests that at least 40 percent of children with early depressive experience do not have recurrences. This, of course, suggests that resilience factors function to moderate or mitigate continuity in depressive experience. Resilient processes associated with depression in childhood are complex (Shannon et al., 2007), but likely many factors operate to affect the continuity of child depressive experience, including child sex, SES, psychophysiological markers, comorbid anxiety, and the presence of parental psychopathology, to list a few. Continued attention to the complex pathways of influence that operate to create, maintain, and possibly mitigate child depressive experiences over time is much needed. The same would be true for understanding parental depression and its effects over time, especially for periods that extend beyond the early postnatal phases.

A substantial growth in research has addressed depression in both child and parent contexts, and the nature, risk, and consequences of depression in children's lives have become much better understood than ever before. Family system–level processes, however, have not received the same attention to date despite the fact that the depression that affects children's lives can reside in both children and parents. Marital relationships, coparenting, family organization and dynamics, sibling relationships, multigenerational caregiving, and other family system processes all influence or are influenced by the presence of depression in one or more family members. Taraban and colleagues (2017), for example, found that marital quality moderated the relation between maternal depression and parenting but in unanticipated ways, such that relations between maternal depression and parenting were strongest when marital quality was higher. In a study exploring connections between parents' depressive trajectories, Kiviruusu and colleagues (2020) reported that maternal and paternal trajectories were positively associated, and the predictors of those trajectories were common to both. Complex relations were also found for a study in which less positive coparenting was associated with depression for both mothers and fathers (Williams, 2018), but crossover effects were observed from paternal depression to maternal coparenting. Similar systemic complexities were reported by Tissot and colleagues (2017) in a study of Swiss parents of infants in which fathers' coparenting mediated the relation between maternal depression and children's behavior problems during toddlerhood, as maternal depression was associated with lower coparenting support and greater problems in toddler behavior.

The few studies that have addressed family system issues have been instructive and encourage deeper and more extensive future investigation. The efforts that address family systems so far, however, have focused more on parent depression than child depressive experience. Nonetheless, these studies suggest that taking a more systemic view of the pathways that operate within the family system will add important texture to current perspectives on depression in children's lives, especially if they expand to focus on depressive experience in the child.

Our knowledge base about depression in children's lives is vast, and it is expanding. Our models of etiology, continuity, consequences, and intervention are becoming more complex to better reflect the nature of this phenomenon, especially as it focuses on depressive experience that extends from brief mild symptom states to severe depressive disorder in both children and parents. Although depressive experience can be adaptive and contribute to the rich emotional lives of children, the pathways to problematic outcomes must be a continued focus of study to facilitate deeper understandings of depression during childhood and support the development of effective preventive interventions.

References

Abela, J. R., & Hankin, B. L. (2008). Cognitive vulnerability to depression in children and adolescents: A developmental psychopathology perspective. In J. R. Abela & B. L. Hankin (Eds.), *Handbook of depression in children and adolescents*. New York: Guilford Press, pp. 35–78.

Abela, J. R., & Sarin, S. (2002). Cognitive vulnerability to hopelessness depression: A chain is only as strong as its weakest link. *Cognitive Therapy and Research*, *26*(6), 811–29.

Abramson, L. Y., Alloy, L. B., & Metalsky, G. I. (1995). Hopelessness depression. In G. M. Buchanan & M. E. P. Seligman (Eds.), *Explanatory style*. Hillsdale, NJ: Lawrence Erlbaum Associates, pp. 113–34.

Acevedo-Garcia, D., McArdle, N., Hardy, E. F. et al. (2014). The child opportunity index: Improving collaboration between community development and public health. *Health Affairs*, *33*(11), 1948–57.

Adam, E. K., Doane, L. D., Zinbarg, R. E., Mineka, S., Craske, M. G., & Griffith, J. W. (2010). Prospective prediction of major depressive disorder from cortisol awakening responses in adolescence. *Psychoneuroendocrinology*, *35*(6), 921–31.

Adams, P., Abela, J. R., & Hankin, B. L. (2007). Factorial categorization of depression-related constructs in early adolescents. *Journal of Cognitive Psychotherapy*, *21*(2), 123–39. https://doi.org/10.1891/088983907780851540

Adkins, D. E., Wang, V., & Elder, G. H., Jr. (2009). Structure and stress: Trajectories of depressive symptoms across adolescence and young adulthood. *Social Forces; a Scientific Medium of Social Study and Interpretation*, *88*(1), 31–60. https://doi.org/10.1353/sof.0.0238

Agoston, A. M., & Rudolph, K. D. (2013). Pathways from depressive symptoms to low social status. *Journal of Abnormal Child Psychology*, *41*(2), 295–308. https://doi.org/10.1007/s10802-012-9675-y

Ahun, M. N., Geoffroy, M., Herba, C. M. et al. (2017). Timing and chronicity of maternal depression symptoms and children's verbal abilities. *The Journal of Pediatrics*, *190*, 251–57. https://doi.org/10.1016/j.jpeds.2017.07.007

Aldao, A., Gee, D. G., De Los Reyes, A., & Seager, I. (2016). Emotion regulation as a transdiagnostic factor in the development of internalizing and externalizing psychopathology: Current and future directions. *Development and Psychopathology*, *28*(4pt1), 927–46. https://doi.org/10.1017/S0954579416000638

American Psychiatric Association. (2013). *Diagnostic and statistical manual of mental disorders* (5th ed.). Arlington, VA: American Psychiatric Association. https://doi.org/10.1176/appi.books.9780890425559

Anderson, E. R., & Hope, D. A. (2008). A review of the tripartite model for understanding the link between anxiety and depression in youth. *Clinical Psychology Review, 28*(2), 275–87. https://doi.org/10.1016/j.cpr.2007.05.004

Angold, A., Erkanli, A., Farmer, E. M. Z. et al. (2002). Psychiatric disorder, impairment, and service use in rural African American and white youth. *Archives of General Psychiatry, 59*(10), 893–904. https://doi.org/10.1001/archpsyc.59.10.893

Arifin, S., Cheyne, H., & Maxwell, M. (2018). Review of the prevalence of postnatal depression across cultures. *AIMS Public Health, 5*(3), 260–95. https://doi.org/10.3934/publichealth.2018.3.260

Auerbach, R. P., Eberhart, N. K., & Abela, J. R. Z. (2010). Cognitive vulnerability to depression in Canadian and Chinese adolescents. *Journal of Abnormal Child Psychology, 38*(1), 57–68. https://doi.org/10.1007/s10802-009-9344-y

Augustine, J. M., & Crosnoe, R. (2010). Mothers' depression and educational attainment and their children's academic trajectories. *Journal of Health and Social Behavior, 51*(3), 274–90. https://doi.org/10.1177/0022146510377757

Austin, A. A., & Chorpita, B. F. (2004). Temperament, anxiety, and depression: Comparisons across five ethnic groups of children. *Journal of Clinical Child and Adolescent Psychology, 33*(2), 216–26.

Avenevoli, S., Knight, E., Kessler, R. C., & Merikangas, K. R. (2008). Epidemiology of depression in children and adolescents. In J. R. Z. Abela & B. L. Hankin (Eds.), *Handbook of depression in children and adolescents*, New York: Guilford Press, pp. 6–34.

Azaka, S., & Raeder, S. (2013). Trajectories of parenting behavior and maternal depression. *Infant Behavior and Development, 36*(3), 391–402. https://doi.org/10.1016/j.infbeh.2013.03.004

Bachmann, C. J., Aagaard, L., Burcu, M. et al. (2016). Trends and patterns of antidepressant use in children and adolescents from five western countries, 2005–2012. *European Neuropsychopharmacology: The Journal of the European College of Neuropsychopharmacology, 26*(3), 411–19. https://doi.org/10.1016/j.euroneuro.2016.02.001

Baker, C., & Kuhn, L. (2018). Mediated pathways from maternal depression and early parenting to children's executive function and externalizing behaviour problems. *Infant and Child Development, 27*(1), 1–12. https://doi.org/10.1002/icd.2052

Ballard, C., & Davies, R., (1996). Postnatal depression in fathers. *International Review of Psychiatry, 8*(1), 65–71.

Barajas-Gonzalez, R. G., & Brooks-Gunn, J. (2014). Income, neighborhood stressors, and harsh parenting: Test of moderation by ethnicity, age, and gender. *Journal of Family Psychology, 28*(6), 855–66. https://doi.org/10.1037/a0038242

Barker, D. J. (2007). The origins of the developmental origins theory. *Journal of Internal Medicine, 261*(5), 412–17.

Barrett, K. C. & Campos, J. J. (1987). Perspectives on emotional development II: A functionalist approach to emotions. In J. D. Osofsky (Ed.), *Handbook of infant development*. New York: Guilford Press, pp. 555–78.

Bates, J. E., Schermerhorn, A. C., & Petersen, I. T. (2012). Temperament and parenting in developmental perspective. In M. Zentner & R. L. Shiner (Eds.), *Handbook of temperament*. New York: Guilford Press, pp. 425–41.

Bauer, A. M., Quas, J. A., & Boyce, W. T. (2002). Associations between physiological reactivity and children's behavior: Advantages of a multisystem approach. *Journal of Developmental and Behavioral Pediatrics, 23*(2), 102–13.

Beardselee, W. R., Versage, E. M., & Giadstone, T. R. (1998). Children of affectively ill parents: A review of the past 10 years. *Journal of the American Academy of Child and Adolescent Psychiatry, 37*(11), 1134–41.

Beauchaine, T. P. (2015). Respiratory sinus arrhythmia: A transdiagnostic biomarker of emotion dysregulation and psychopathology. *Current Opinion in Psychology, 3*, 43–47.

Beauchaine, T. P., & Hinshaw, S. P. (2020). RDoC and psychopathology among youth: Misplaced assumptions and an agenda for future research. *Journal of Clinical Child and Adolescent Psychology, 49*(3), 322–40. https://doi.org/10.1080/15374416.2020.1750022

Beauchaine, T. P., & Tackett, J. L. (2020). Irritability as a transdiagnostic vulnerability trait: Current issues and future directions. *Behavior Therapy, 51*(2), 350–64. https://doi.org/10.1016/j.beth.2019.10.009

Beauchaine, T. P., & Thayer, J. F. (2015). Heart rate variability as a transdiagnostic biomarker of psychopathology. *International Journal of Psychophysiology, 98*(2pt 2), 338–50. https://doi.org/10.1016/j.ijpsycho.2015.08.004

Beaujean, A. A., Parker, S., & Qui, X. (2013). The relationship between cognitive ability and depression: A longitudinal data analysis. *Social Psychiatry and Psychiatric Epidemiology, 48*(12), 1983–92. https://doi.org/10.1007/s00127-013-0668-0

Beck, A. T. (2008). The evolution of the cognitive model of depression and its neurobiological correlates. *American Journal of Psychiatry, 165*(8), 969–77.

Beeghly, M., Weinberg, M. K., Olson, K. L., Kernan, H., Riley, J., & Tronick, E. Z. (2002). Stability and change in level of maternal depressive symptomatology during the first postpartum year. *Journal of Affective Disorders, 71*(1–3), 169–80.

Belden, A. C., Pagliaccio, D., Murphy, E. R., Luby, J. L., & Barch, D. M. (2015). Neural activation during cognitive emotion regulation in previously depressed compared to healthy children: Evidence of specific alterations. *Journal of the American Academy of Child and Adolescent Psychiatry, 54*(9), 771–81. https://doi.org/10.1016/j.jaac.2015.06.014

Belsky, J., & Pluess, M. (2009). Beyond diathesis stress: Differential susceptibility to environmental influences. *Psychological Bulletin, 135*(6), 885–908. https://doi.org/10.1037/a0017376

Benner, A. D., & Mistry, R. S. (2020). Child development during the COVID-19 pandemic through a life course theory lens. *Child Development Perspectives,* 14(4), 236–43. https://doi.org/10.1111/cdep.12387

Berdan, L. E., Keane, S. P., & Calkins, S. D. (2008). Temperament and externalizing behavior: Social preference and perceived acceptance as protective factors. *Developmental Psychology, 44*(4), 957–68.

Bernard, K., Nissim, G., Vaccaro, S., Harris, J. L., & Lindhiem, O. (2018). Association between maternal depression and maternal sensitivity from birth to 12 months: A meta-analysis. *Attachment and Human Development, 20*(6), 578–99. https://doi.org/10.1080/14616734.2018.1430839

Berntson, G. G., Cacioppo, J. T., Quigley, K. S., & Fabro, V. T. (1994). Autonomic space and psychophysiological response. *Psychophysiology, 31*(1), 44–61.

Bilsky, S. A., Cole, D. A., Dukewich, T. L. et al. (2013). Does supportive parenting mitigate the longitudinal effects of peer victimization on depressive thoughts and symptoms in children? *Journal of Abnormal Psychology, 122* (2), 406–19. https://doi.org/10.1037/a0032501

Bonapersona, V., Joëls, M., & Sarabdjitsingh, R. A. (2018). Effects of early life stress on biochemical indicators of the dopaminergic system: A 3 level meta-analysis of rodent studies. *Neuroscience and Biobehavioral Reviews, 95*, 1–16. https://doi.org/10.1016/j.neubiorev.2018.09.003

Bornstein, M. H. (2013). Mother-infant attunement: A multilevel approach via body, brain, and behavior. In M. Legerstee, D. W. Haley, & M. H. Bornstein (Eds.), *The infant mind: Origins of the social brain.* New York: Guilford Press, pp. 266–98.

Bornstein, M. H. (2021). Introduction: The SARS-CoV-2 pandemic: Issues for families, parents, and children. In M. H. Bornstein (Ed.), *Psychological insights for understanding Covid-19 and families, parents, and children*. New York: Routledge, pp. 1–70.

Bornstein, M. H., Arterberry, M. E., Mash, C., & Manian, N. (2011). Discrimination of facial expression by 5-month-old infants of nondepressed and clinically depressed mothers. *Infant Behavior and Development, 34*(1), 100–6. https://doi.org/10.1016/j.infbeh.2010.10.002

Bornstein, M. H., & Cote, L. R. (2009). Child temperament in three U.S. cultural groups. *Infant Mental Health Journal, 30*(5), 433–51. https://doi.org/10.1002/imhj.20223

Bornstein, M. H., Hahn, C.-S., & Suwalsky, J. T. D. (2013). Language and internalizing and externalizing behavioral adjustment: Developmental pathways from childhood to adolescence. *Development and Psychopathology, 25*, 857–78. https://doi.org/10.1017/S0954579413000217

Bornstein, M. H., Henry, L. M., & Manian, N. (in press). Language development in children of clinically depressed mothers in remission: Early experience effects. *Developmental Psychology*.

Bornstein, M. H., Mash, C., Arterberry, M. E., & Manian, N. (2012). Object perception in 5-month-old infants of clinically depressed and nondepressed mothers. *Infant Behavior and Development, 35*(1), 150–57. https://doi.org/10.1016/j.infbeh.2011.07.008

Bornstein, M. H., Putnick, D. L., & Esposito, G. (2017). Continuity and stability in development. *Child development Perspectives, 11*(2), 113–19. https://doi.org/10.1111/cdep.12221

Bosch, N. M., Riese, H., Ormel, J., Verhulst, F., & Oldehinkel, A. J. (2009). Stressful life events and depressive symptoms in young adolescents: Modulation by respiratory sinus arrhythmia? The TRAILS study. *Biological Psychology, 81*(1), 40–47.

Bose, D., & Pettit, J. W. (2018). Depression. In S. Hupp (Ed.), *Child and adolescent psychotherapy: Components of evidence-based treatments for youth and their parents*. New York: Cambridge University Press, pp. 138–53.

Boyce, W. T., Quas, J., Alkon, A., Smider, N. A., Essex, M. J., & Kupfer, D. J. (2001). Autonomic reactivity and psychopathology in middle childhood. *The British Journal of Psychiatry: The Journal of Mental Science, 179*, 144–50.

Braungart-Rieker, J. M., Hill-Soderlund, A. L., & Karrass, J. (2010). Fear and anger reactivity trajectories from 4 to 16 months: The roles of temperament, regulation, and maternal sensitivity. *Developmental Psychology, 46*(4), 791–804. https://doi.org/10.1037/a0019673

Braungart-Rieker, J. M., Zentall, S., Lickenbrock, D. M., Ekas, N. V., Oshio, T., & Planalp, E. (2014). Attachment in the making: Mother and father sensitivity and infants' responses during the Still-Face Paradigm. *Journal of Experimental Child Psychology*, *125*, 63–84. https://doi.org/10.1016/j .jecp.2014.02.007

Brazelton, T. B., Tronick, E., Adamson, L., Als, H., & Wise, S. (1975). Early mother-infant reciprocity. In *Parent-infant interaction*, Ciba Foundation Symposium 33, New York: Elsevier, pp. 137–54.

Brendgen, M., Vitaro, F., Turgeon, L., & Poulin, F. (2002). Assessing aggressive and depressed children's social relations with classmates and friends: A matter of perspective. *Journal of Abnormal Child Psychology*, *30*(6), 609–24. https://doi.org/10.1023/A: 1020863730902

Bridge, J. A., Iyengar, S., Salary, C. B. et al. (2007). Clinical response and risk for reported suicidal ideation and suicide attempts in pediatric antidepressant treatment: A meta-analysis of randomized controlled trials. *Journal of the American Medical Association*, *297*(15), 1683–96. https://doi.org/10.1001 /jama.297.15.1683

Bronfenbrenner, U., & Morris, P. A. (2007). The bioecological model of human development. In W. Damon & R. M. Lerner (Eds.), *Handbook of child psychology: Theoretical models of human development*, 6th ed. New York: Wiley, pp. 793–828. https://doi.org/10.1002/9780470147658 .chpsy0114

Brooks, B. L., Iverson, G. L., Sherman, E. M., & Roberge, M. C. (2010). Identifying cognitive problems in children and adolescents with depression using computerized neuropsychological testing. *Applied Neuropsychology*, *17*(1), 37–43.

Bufferd, S. J., Dougherty, L. R., & Olino, T. M. (2017). Mapping the frequency and severity of depressive behaviors in preschool-aged children. *Child Psychiatry and Human Development*, *48*(6), 934–43. https://doi.org/10 .1007/s10578-017-0715-2

Burke, H. M., Davis, M. C., Otte, C., & Mohr, D. C. (2005). Depression and cortisol responses to psychological stress: A meta-analysis. *Psychoneuroendocrinology*, *30*(9), 846–56. https://doi.org/10.1016/j .psyneuen.2005.02.010

Calvete, E., Villardón, L., & Estévez, A. (2008). Attributional style and depressive symptoms in adolescents: An examination of the role of various indicators of cognitive vulnerability. *Behaviour Research and Therapy*, *46*(8), 944–53.

Campbell, S. B., Morgan-Lopez, A., Cox, M. J., & McLoyd, V. C. (2009). A latent class analysis of maternal depressive symptoms over 12 years and offspring adjustment in adolescence. *Journal of Abnormal Psychology, 118* (3), 479–93. https://doi.org/10.1037/a001592

Carnegie, R., Araya, R., Ben-Shlomo, Y. et al. (2014). Cortisol awakening response and subsequent depression: prospective longitudinal study. *British Journal of Psychiatry, 204*(2), 137–43. https://doi.org/10.1192/bjp .bp.113.126250

Carpenter, T., Grecian, S. M., & Reynolds, R. M. (2017). Sex differences in early-life programming of the hypothalamic–pituitary–adrenal axis in humans suggest increased vulnerability in females: A systematic review. *Journal of Developmental Origins of Health and Disease, 8*(2), 244–55. https://doi.org/10.1017/S204017441600074X

Cataldo, M. G., Nobile, M., Lorusso, M. L., Battaglia, M., & Molteni, M. (2005). Impulsivity in depressed children and adolescents: A comparison between behavioral and neuropsychological data. *Psychiatry Research, 136* (2–3), 123–33.

Chae, D. H., Clouston, S., Martz, C. D. et al. (2018). Area racism and birth outcomes among Blacks in the United States. *Social Science and Medicine, 199*, 49–55. https://doi.org/10.1016/j.socscimed.2017.04.019

Chang, L., Schwartz, D., Dodge, K. A., & McBride-Chang, C. (2003). Harsh parenting in relation to child emotion regulation and aggression. *Journal of Family Psychology, 17*(4), 598–606. https://doi.org/10.1037/0893-3200 .17.4.598

Chen, J. J. L., & Liu, X. (2012). The mediating role of perceived parental warmth and parental punishment in the psychological well-being of children in rural China. *Social Indicators Research, 107*(3), 483–508. https://doi.org /10.1007/s11205-011-9859-9

Chess, S., & Thomas, A. (1999). *Goodness of fit: Clinical applications from infancy through adult life*. Philadelphia, PA: Brunner/Mazel.

Cheung, K., & Theule, J. (2019). Paternal depression and child externalizing behaviors: A meta-analysis. *Journal of Family Psychology, 33*(1), 98–108. https://doi.org/10.1037/fam0000473

Choukas-Bradley, S., & Prinstein, M. J. (2014). Peer relationships and the development of psychopathology. In M. Lewis & K. D. Rudolph (Eds.), *Handbook of developmental psychopathology*. New York: Springer Science + Business Media, pp. 185–204. https://doi.org/10.1007/978-1-4614-9608-3

Cicchetti, D. (2006). Development and psychopathology. In D. Cicchetti & D. J. Cohen (Eds.), *Developmental psychopathology, Vol. 1: Theory and method*, 2nd ed. Hoboken, NJ: Wiley, pp. 1–23.

Cicchetti, D, Rogosch, F. A., & Toth, S. L. (1994). A developmental psycho-pathology perspective on depression in children and adolescents. In

W. M. Reynolds & H. F. Johnston (Eds.), *Handbook of depression in children and adolescents*. Issues in clinical child psychology. New York: Plenum Press, pp. 123–41.

Cicchetti, D., & Toth, S. L. (1998). The development of depression in children and adolescents. *American Psychologist, 53*(2), 221–41. https://doi.org/10 .1037/0003-066X.53.2.221

Cipriani, A., Zhou, X., Del Giovane, C. et al. (2016). Comparative efficacy and tolerability of antidepressants for major depressive disorder in children and adolescents: A network meta-analysis. *The Lancet, 388*(10047), 881–90. doi.10.1016/S0140-6736(16)30385-3

Clark, L. A., Watson, D., & Mineka, S. (1994). Temperament, personality, and the mood and anxiety disorders. *Journal of Abnormal Psychology, 103*(1), 103–16.

Clifford, S., Lemery-Chalfant, K., & Goldsmith, H. H. (2015). The unique and shared genetic and environmental contributions to fear, anger, and sadness in childhood. *Child Development, 86*(5), 1538–56. https://doi.org/10.1111/cdev .12394

Cohen, J. R., Andrews, A. R., Davis, M. M., & Rudolph, K. D. (2018). Anxiety and depression during childhood and adolescence: Testing theoretical models of continuity and discontinuity. *Journal of Abnormal Child Psychology, 46* (6), 1295–1308. https://doi.org/10.1007/s10802-017-0370-x

Cohen, S., Kessler, R. C., & Gordon, L. U. (1995). Strategies for measuring stress in studies of psychiatric and physical disorders. In S Cohen, R. Kessler, & L. Gordon (Eds.), *Measuring stress: A guide for health and social scientists*. New York: Oxford University Press, pp. 3–26.

Cole, P. M. (2016). Emotion and the development of psychopathology. In D. Cicchetti (Ed.), *Developmental psychopathology, Vol. 1: Theory and method*, 3rd ed. Hoboken, NJ: Wiley, pp. 265–324. https://doi.org/10.1002 /9781119125556.devpsy107

Cole, D. A., Dukewich, T. L., Roeder, K. et al. (2014). Linking peer victimization to the development of depressive self-schemas in children and adolescents. *Journal of Abnormal Child Psychology, 42*(1), 149–60. https:// doi.org/10.1007/s10802-013-9769-1

Cole, D. A., Martin, J. M., & Powers, B. (1997). A competency-based model of child depression: A longitudinal study of peer, parent, teacher, and self-evaluations. *Journal of Child Psychology and Psychiatry, 38*(5), 505– 14. https://doi.org/10.1111/j.1469-7610.1997.tb01537.x

Cole, D. A., Peeke, L. G., Martin, J. M., Truglio, R., & Seroczynski, A. D. (1998). A longitudinal look at the relation between depression and anxiety in children and adolescents. *Journal of Consulting and Clinical Psychology, 66* (3), 451–60. https://doi.org/10.1037/0022-006X.66.3.451

Cole, D. A., Sinclair-McBride, K. R., Zelkowitz, R., Bilsk, S. A., Roeder, K., & Spinelli, T. (2016). Peer victimization and harsh parenting predict cognitive diatheses for depression in children and adolescents. *Journal of Clinical Child and Adolescent Psychology, 45*(5), 668–80. https://doi.org/10.1080/15374416.2015.1004679

Cole, D. A., & Turner, J. E. (1993). Models of cognitive mediation and moderation in child depression. *Journal of Abnormal Psychology, 102*(2), 271–81.

Compas, B. E., Connor-Smith, J., & Jaser, S. S. (2004). Temperament, stress reactivity, and coping: Implications for depression in childhood and adolescence. *Journal of Clinical Child and Adolescent Psychology, 33*(1), 21–31.

Compas, B. E., Ey, S., & Grant, K. E. (1993). Taxonomy, assessment, and diagnosis of depression during adolescence. *Psychological Bulletin, 114*(2), 323–44. https://doi.org/10.1037/0033-2909.114.2.323

Conger, R. D., Wallace, L. E., Sun, Y., Simons, R. L., McLoyd, V. C., & Brody, G. H. (2002). Economic pressure in African American families: A replication and extension of the family stress model. *Developmental Psychology, 38*(2), 179–93. https://doi.org/10.1037/0012-1649.38.2.179

Conley, C. S., Haines, B. A., Hilt, L. M., & Metalsky, G. I. (2001). The children's attributional style interview: Developmental tests of cognitive diathesis-stress theories of depression. *Journal of Abnormal Child Psychology, 29*(5), 445–63. https://doi.org/10.1023/A: 1010451604161

Connell, A. M., & Goodman, S. H. (2002). The association between psychopathology in fathers versus mothers and children's internalizing and externalizing behavior problems: A meta-analysis. *Psychological Bulletin, 128* (5), 746–73. https://doi.org/org/10.1037/0033-2909.128.5.746

Copeland, W. E., Angold, A., Costello, E. J., & Egger, H. (2013). Prevalence, comorbidity, and correlates of DSM-5 proposed disruptive mood dysregulation disorder. *American Journal of Psychiatry, 170*(2), 173–79.

Coplan, R. J., Gavinski-Molina, M. H., Lagacé-Séguin, D. G., & Wichmann, C. (2001). When girls versus boys play alone: Nonsocial play and adjustment in kindergarten. *Developmental Psychology, 37*(4), 464–74. https://doi.org/10.1037/0012-1649.37.4.464

Cornish, A. M., McMahon, C. A., Ungerer, J. A., Barnett, B., Kowalenko, N., & Tennant, C. (2005). Postnatal depression and infant cognitive and motor development in the second postnatal year: The impact of depression chronicity and infant gender. *Infant Behavior and Development, 28*(4), 407–17. https://doi.org/10.1016/j.infbeh.2005.03.004

Costello, E. J., Farmer, E. M. Z., Angold, A., Burns, B. J., & Erkanli, A. (1997). Psychiatric disorders among American Indian and white youth in

Appalachia: The great smoky mountains study. *American Journal of Public Health, 87*(5), 827–32. https://doi.org/10.2105/AJPH.87.5.827

Crick, N. R., & Ladd, G. W. (1993). Children's perceptions of their peer experiences: Attributions, loneliness, social anxiety, and social avoidance. *Developmental Psychology, 29*(2), 244–54. https://doi.org/10.1037/0012-1649.29.2.244

Crowe, K., & McKay, D. (2017). Efficacy of cognitive-behavioral therapy for childhood anxiety and depression. *Journal of Anxiety Disorders, 49*, 76–87. https://doi.org/10.1016/j.janxdis.2017.04.001

Culpin, I., Stapinski, L., Miles, Ö. B., Araya, R., & Joinson, C. (2015). Exposure to socioeconomic adversity in early life and risk of depression at 18 years: The mediating role of locus of control. *Journal of Affective Disorders, 183*, 269–78. https://doi.org/10.1016/j.jad.2015.05.030

Cummings, E. M., Cheung, R. Y. M., & Davies, P. T. (2013). Prospective relations between parental depression, negative expressiveness, emotional insecurity, and children's internalizing symptoms. *Child Psychiatry and Human Development, 44*(6), 698–708. https://doi.org/10.1007/s10578-013-0362-1

Cummings, E. M., Keller, P. S., & Davies, P. T. (2005). Towards a family process model of maternal and paternal depressive symptoms: Exploring multiple relations with child and family functioning. *Journal of Child Psychology and Psychiatry, 46*(5), 479–89. https://doi.org/10.1111/j.1469-7610.2004.00368.x

Cummings, E. M., Merrilees, C. E., & George, M. W. (2010). Fathers, marriages, and families: Revisiting and updating the framework for fathering in family context. In M. E. Lamb (Ed.), *The role of the father in child development* (5th ed.). Hoboken, NJ: Wiley, pp. 154–76.

Dallaire, D. H., Pineda, A. Q., Cole, D. A. et al. (2006). Relation of positive and negative parenting to children's depressive symptoms. *Journal of Clinical Child and Adolescent Psychology, 35*(2), 313–22 https://doi.org/10.1207/s15374424jccp3502_15

Davé, S., Petersen, I, Sherr, L., & Nazareth, I. (2010). Incidence of maternal and paternal depression in primary care: A cohort study using a primary care database. *Archives of Pediatric and Adolescent Medicine, 164*(11), 1038–44. https://doi.org/10.1001/archpediatrics.2010.184

David-Ferdon, C., & Kaslow, N. J. (2008). Evidence-based psychosocial treatments for child and adolescent depression. *Journal of Clinical Child and Adolescent Psychology, 37*(1), 62–104. https://doi.org/10.1080/15374410701817865

Davidov, M., & Grusec, J. E. (2006). Untangling the links of parental responsiveness to distress and warmth to child outcomes. *Child Development, 77*(1), 44–58. https://doi.org/10.1300/J002v34n03_05

Davidson, R. J., Pizzagalli, D. A., & Nitschke, J. B. (2009). Representation and regulation of emotion in depression: Perspectives from affective neuroscience. In I. H. Gotlib & C. Hammen (Eds.), *Handbook of depression*, 2nd ed. New York: Guilford Press, pp. 218–48.

Davies, P., & Windle, M. (2001). Interparental discord and adolescent adjustment trajectories: The potentiating and protective role of intrapersonal attributes. *Child Development*, *72*(4), 1163–78.

Davis, M., Goodman, S. H., Lavner, J. A. et al. (2019). Patterns of positivity: Positive affect trajectories among infants of mothers with a history of depression. *Infancy*, *24*(6), 911–32. https://doi.org/10.1111/Infa.12314.

De Bolle, M., & De Fruyt, F. (2010). The tripartite model in childhood and adolescence: Future directions for developmental research. *Child Development Perspectives*, *4*(3), 174–80. https://doi.org/10.1111/j.1750-8606.2010.00136.x

Dekker, M. C., Ferdinand, R. F., van Lang, N. D. J., Bongers, I. L., van der Ende, J., & Verhulst, F. C. (2007). Developmental trajectories of depressive symptoms from early childhood to late adolescence: Gender differences and adult outcome. *Journal of Child Psychology and Psychiatry*, *48*(7), 657–66. https://doi.org/10.1111/j.1469-7610.2007.01742.x

Del Giudice, M., Ellis, B. J., & Shirtcliff, E. A. (2011). The Adaptive Calibration Model of stress responsivity. *Neuroscience and Biobehavioral Reviews*, *35*(7), 1562–92. https://doi.org/10.1016/j.neubiorev.2010.11.007

Del Giudice, M., Hinnant, J. B., Ellis, B. J., & El-Sheikh, M. (2012). Adaptive patterns of stress responsivity: A preliminary investigation. *Developmental Psychology*, *48*(3), 775–90. https://doi.org/10.1037/a0026519

Denham, S. A., Bassett, H. H., & Wyatt, T. (2015). The socialization of emotional competence. In J. E. Grusec & P. D. Hastings (Eds.), *Handbook of socialization: Theory and research* (2nd ed.). New York: Guilford Press, pp. 590–613.

DeRose, L. M., Shiyko, M., Levey, S., Helm, J., & Hastings, P. D. (2014). Early maternal depression and social skills in adolescence: A marginal structural modeling approach. *Social Development*, *23*(4), 753–69.

Dhillon, A., Sparkes, E., & Duarte, R. V. (2017). Mindfulness-based interventions during pregnancy: A systematic review and meta-analysis. *Mindfulness*, *8*(6), 1421–37. https://doi.org/10.1007/s12671-017-0726-x

Dietz, L. J., Weinberg, R. J., Brent, D. A., & Mufson, L. (2015). Family-based interpersonal psychotherapy for depressed preadolescents: Examining efficacy and potential treatment mechanisms. *Journal of the American Academy of Child and Adolescent Psychiatry*, *54*(3), 191–99. https://doi.org/10.1016/j.jaac.2014.12.011

Dodge, K. A. (1993). Social-cognitive mechanisms in the development of conduct disorder and depression. *Annual Review of Psychology*, *44*, 559–84.

Doom, J. R., & Cicchetti, D. (2018). The developmental psychopathology of stress exposure in childhood. In K. Harkness & E. Hayden (Eds.), *The Oxford handbook of stress and mental health*. New York: Oxford University Press, pp. 265–85.

Dougherty, L. R., Klein, D. N., Durbin, C. E., Hayden, E. P., & Olino, T. M. (2010). Temperamental positive and negative emotionality and children's depressive symptoms: A longitudinal prospective study from age three to age ten. *Journal of Social and Clinical Psychology*, *29*(4), 462–88. https://doi.org//10.1521/jscp.2010.29.4.462

Doyle, C., & Cicchetti, D. (2018). Future directions in prenatal stress research: Challenges and opportunities related to advancing our understanding of prenatal developmental origins of risk for psychopathology. *Development and Psychopathology*, *30*(3), 721–24. https://doi.org/10.1017/S095457941800069X

Drury, S. S., Scaramella, L., & Zeanah, C. H. (2016). The neurobiological impact of postpartum maternal depression: Prevention and intervention approaches. *Child and Adolescent Psychiatric Clinics of North America*, *25*(2), 179–200. https://doi.org/10.1016/j.chc.2015.11.001

Egger, H. L., & Angold, A. (2009). Classification of psychopathology in early childhood. In C. H. Zeanah, Jr. (Ed.), *Handbook of infant mental health* (3rd ed.). New York: Guilford Press, pp. 285–300.

Eisenberg, N., Cumberland, A., & Spinrad, T. L. (1998). Parental socialization of emotion. *Psychological Inquiry*, *9*(4), 241–73. https://doi.org/10.1207/s15327965pli0904_1

Eisenberg, N., Pidada, S., & Liew, J. (2001). The relations of regulation and negative emotionality to Indonesian children's social functioning. *Child Development*, *72*(6), 1747–63. https://doi.org/10.1111/1467-8624.00376

Ellis, B. J., Boyce, W. T., Belsky, J., Bakermans-Kranenburg, M. J., & Van Ijzendoorn, M. H. (2011). Differential susceptibility to the environment: An evolutionary–neurodevelopmental theory. *Development and Psychopathology*, *23*(1), 7–28. https://doi.org/10.1017/s0954579410000611

Ellis, B. J., Oldehinkel, A. J., & Nederhof, E. (2017). The adaptive calibration model of stress responsivity: An empirical test in the Tracking Adolescents' Individual Lives Survey study. *Development and Psychopathology*, *29*(3), 1001–21. https://doi.org/10.1017/s0954579416000985

Emerson, C. S., Mollet, G. A., & Harrison, D. W. (2005). Anxious-depression in boys: An evaluation of executive functioning. *Archives of Clinical Neuropsychology: The Official Journal of the National Academy of*

Neuropsychologists, 20(4), 539–46. https://doi.org/10.1016/j.acn.2004.10.003

Evans, G. W., Li, D., & Whipple, S. S. (2013). Cumulative risk and child development. *Psychological Bulletin, 139*(6), 1342–96.

Evans, J., Melotti, R., Heron, J. et al. (2012). The timing of maternal depressive symptoms and child cognitive development: A longitudinal study. *Journal of Child Psychology and Psychiatry, 53*(6), 632–40. https://doi.org/10.1111/j.1469-7610.2011.02513.x

Fauber, R., Forehand, R., Long, N., Burke, M., & Faust, J. (1987). The relationship of young adolescent children's depression inventory (CDI) scores to their social and cognitive functioning. *Journal of Psychopathology and Behavioral Assessment, 9* (2), 161–72.

Feldman, R. (2003). Infant–mother and infant–father synchrony: The coregulation of positive arousal. *Infant Mental Health Journal, 24*(1), 1–23. https://doi.org/10.1002/imhj.10041

Feldman, R. (2007a). Parent-infant synchrony and the construction of shared timing; physiological precursors, developmental outcomes, and risk conditions. *Journal of Child Psychology and Psychiatry, 48*(3–4), 329–54. https://doi.org/10.1111/j.1469-7610.2006.01701.x

Feldman, R. (2007b). Maternal versus child risk and the development of parent-child and family relationships in five high-risk populations. *Development and Psychopathology, 19*(2), 293–312.

Feng, X., Shaw, D. S., Skuban, E. M., & Lane, T. (2007). Emotional exchange in mother-child dyads: Stability, mutual influence, and associations with maternal depression and child problem behavior. *Journal of Family Psychology, 21* (4), 714–25. https://doi.org/10.1037/0893-3200.21.4.714

Fergusson, D. M. & Horwood, L. J. (2003). Resilience to childhood adversity: Results of a 12-year study. In S. S. Luthar (Ed.), *Resilience and vulnerability: Adaptation in the context of childhood adversities.* New York: Cambridge University Press, pp. 130–55. https://doi.org/10.1017/CBO9780511615788.008

Field, T. (1994). The effects of mother's physical and emotional unavailability on emotion regulation. *Monographs of the Society for Research in Child Development, 59* (2–3), 208–27, 250–83. https://doi.org/10.2307/1166147

Field, T. (1995). Infants of depressed mothers. *Infant Behavior and Development, 18*(1), 1–13.

Finkelhor, D., Shattuck, A., Turner, H., & Hamby, S. (2013). Improving the adverse childhood experiences study scale. *The Journal of the American Medical Association Pediatrics, 167*(1), 70–75. https://doi.org/10.1001/jamapediatrics.2013.420

Fonseca, A., Alves, S., Monteiro, F., Gorayeb, R., & Canavarro, M. C. (2020). Be a mom, a web-based intervention to prevent postpartum depression: Results from a pilot randomized controlled trial. *Behavior Therapy, 51*(4), 616–33. https://doi.org/10.1016/j.beth.2019.09.007

Fraley, R. C., Roisman, G. I., & Haltigan, J. D. (2013). The legacy of early experiences in development: Formalizing alternative models of how early experiences are carried forward over time. *Developmental Psychology, 49*(1), 109–26. https://doi.org/10.1037/a0027852

Fredriksen, E., von Soest, T., Smith, L., & Moe, V. (2019). Parenting stress plays a mediating role in the prediction of early child development from both parents' perinatal depressive symptoms. *Journal of Abnormal Child Psychology, 47*(1), 149–64. https://doi.org/10.1007/s10802-018-0428-4

Fristad, M. A., & Black, S. R. (2018). Mood disorders in childhood and adolescence. In J. N. Butcher, & P. C. Kendall (Eds.), *APA handbook of psychopathology: Child and adolescent psychopathology*, Vol. 2. Washington DC: American Psychological Association, pp. 253–77. https://doi.org/10.1037/0000065-013

Gaffrey, M. S., Belden, A. C., & Luby, J. L. (2011). The 2-week duration criterion and severity and course of early childhood depression: Implications for nosology. *Journal of Affective Disorders, 133*(3), 537–45. https://doi.org/10.1016/j.jad.2011.04.056

Garber, J., Ciesla, J. A., McCauley, E., Diamond, G., & Schloredt, K. A. (2011). Remission of depression in parents: Links to healthy functioning in their children. *Child Development, 82*, 226–43.

Garber, J., & Rao, U. (2014). Depression in children and adolescents. In M. Lewis & K. Rudolph (Eds.), *Handbook of developmental psychopathology*. New York: Springer, pp. 489–520.

Garcia Coll, C., Lamberty, G., Jenkins, R. et al. (1996). An integrative model for the study of developmental competencies in minority children. *Child Development, 67*(5), 1891–1914.

Gardner, F., Connell, A., Trentacosta, C. J., Shaw, D. S., Dishion, T. J., & Wilson, M. N. (2009). Moderators of outcome in a brief family-centered intervention for preventing early problem behavior. *Journal of Consulting and Clinical Psychology, 77*(3), 543–53. https://doi.org/10.2307/1130770

Gartstein, M. A., & Fagot, B. I. (2003). Parental depression, parenting and family adjustment, and child effortful control: Explaining externalizing behaviors for preschool children. *Journal of Applied Developmental Psychology, 24*(2), 143–77. https://doi.org/10.1016/S0193-3973(03)00043-1

Gartstein, M. A., & Rothbart, M. K. (2003). Studying infant temperament via the revised infant behavior questionnaire. *Infant Behavior and Development, 26*(1), 64–86. https://doi.org/10.1016/s0163-6383(02)00169-8

Gartstein, M. A., & Skinner, M. K. (2018). Prenatal influences on temperament development: The role of environmental epigenetics. *Development and Psychopathology, 30*(4), 1269–1303.

Gazelle, H., & Ladd, G. W. (2003). Anxious solitude and peer exclusion: A diathesis–stress model of internalizing trajectories in childhood. *Child Development, 74*(1), 257–78. https://doi.org/10.1111/1467-8624.00534

Gibb, B. E., & Abela, J. R. Z. (2008). Emotional abuse, verbal victimization, and the development of children's negative inferential styles and depressive symptoms. *Cognitive Therapy and Research, 32*(2), 161–76. https://doi.org/10.1007/s10608-006-9106-x

Gibb, B. E., & Coles, M. E. (2005). Cognitive vulnerability-stress models of psychopathology: A developmental perspective. In B. Hankin & J. Abela (Eds.), *Development of psychopathology: A vulnerability-stress perspective.* Thousand Oaks, CA: Sage, pp. 104–35. https://doi.org/10.4135/9781452231655.n5

Gjerde, L. C., Eilertsen, E. M., Hannigan, L. J. et al. (2019). Associations between maternal depressive symptoms and risk for offspring early-life psychopathology: The role of genetic and non-genetic mechanisms. *Psychological Medicine, 51*(3),1–9. https://doi.org/10.1017/S0033291719003301

Gjone, H., & Stevenson, J. (1997). A longitudinal twin study of temperament and behavior problems: Common genetic or environmental influences? *Journal of the American Academy of Child and Adolescent Psychiatry, 36* (10), 1448–56. https://doi.org/10.1097/00004583–199710000–00028

Glover, V., & Hill, J. (2012). Sex differences in the programming effects of prenatal stress on psychopathology and stress responses: An evolutionary perspective. *Physiology and Behavior, 106*(5), 736–40. https://doi.org/10.1016/s0165-0327(02)00426-3

Gluckman, P. D., & Hanson, M. A. (2006). The developmental origins of health and disease. In E. M. Wintour & J.A. Owens (Eds.), *Early life origins of health and disease.* New York: Springer, pp. 1–7.

Gong, C., Duan, X., Su, P. et al. (2019). Heightened HPA-axis stress reactivity and accelerated pubertal progression predicts depressive symptoms over 4-year follow up. *Psychoneuroendocrinology, 103*, 259–65. https://doi.org/10.1016/j.psyneuen.2019.02.001

Goodman, J. H. (2004). Paternal postpartum depression, its relationship to maternal postpartum depression, and implications for family health. *Journal of Advanced Nursing, 45*(1), 26–35.

Goodman, S. H. (2010). Challenges to identifying depression in men and women who are parents. *Archives of Pediatric and Adolescent Medicine, 164*(11), 1069–70.

Goodman, S. H. (2020). Intergenerational transmission of depression. *Annual Review of Clinical Psychology,* 16, 213–38. https://doi.org/10.1146/annurev-clinpsy-071519-113915

Goodman, S. H., & Garber, J. (2017). Evidence-based interventions for depressed mothers and their young children. *Child Development, 88*(2), 368–77. https://doi.org/10.1111/cdev.12732

Goodman, S. H., & Gotlib, I. H. (1999). Risk for psychopathology in the children of depressed mothers: A developmental model for understanding mechanisms of transmission. *Psychological Review, 106*(3), 458–90. https://doi.org/10.1037/0033-295X.106.3.458

Goodman, S. H., Rouse, M. H., Connell, A. M., Broth, M. R., Hall, C. M., & Heyward, D. (2011). Maternal depression and child psychopathology: A meta-analytic review. *Clinical Child and Family Psychology Review, 14*(1), 1–27. https://doi.org/10.1007/s10567-010-0080-1

Goodman, S. H., Simon, H. F., Shamblaw, A. L., & Kim, C. Y. (2020). Parenting as a mediator of associations between mothers and children's functioning: A systematic review and meta-analysis. *Journal of Clinical Child and Family Psychology Review, 23*(4), 427–60. https://doi.org/10.1007/s10567-020-00322-4

Grant, K. E., Compas, B. E., Stuhlmacher, A. F., Thurm, A. E., McMahon, S. D., & Halpert, J. A. (2003). Stressors and child and adolescent psychopathology: Moving from markers to mechanisms of risk. *Psychological Bulletin, 129*(3), 447–66.

Grant, K. E., Compas, B. E., Thurm, A. E., McMahon, S. D., & Gipson, P. Y. (2004). Stressors and child and adolescent psychopathology: Measurement issues and prospective effects. *Journal of Clinical Child and Adolescent Psychology, 33*(2), 412–25.

Grant, K. E., Compas, B. E., Thurm, A. E. et al. (2006). Stressors and child and adolescent psychopathology: Evidence of moderating and mediating effects. *Clinical Psychology Review, 26*(3), 257–83.

Gray, S. A. O., Jones, C. W., Theall, K. P., Glackin, E., & Drury, S. S. (2017). Thinking across generations: Unique contributions of maternal early life and prenatal stress to infant physiology. *Journal of the American Academy of Child and Adolescent Psychiatry, 56*(11), 922–29. https://doi.org/10.1016/j.jaac.2017.09.001

Grusec, J. E., & Davidov, M. (2010). Integrating different perspectives on socialization theory and research: A domain-specific approach. *Child Development, 81*(3), 687–709.

Guedeney, A. (2007). Withdrawal behavior and depression in infancy. *Infant Mental Health Journal, 28*(4), 393–408. https://doi.org/10.1002/imhj.20143

Guerry, J. D., & Hastings, P. D. (2011). In search of HPA axis dysregulation in child and adolescent depression. *Clinical Child and Family Psychology Review, 14*(2), 135–60. https://doi.org/10.1007/s10567-011-0084-5

Gunlicks, M. L., & Weissman, M. M. (2008). Change in child psychopathology with improvement in parental depression: A systematic review. *Journal of the American Academy of Child and Adolescent Psychiatry, 47*(4), 379–89.

Guo, L., Zhang, J., Mu, L., & Ye, Z. (2020). Preventing postpartum depression with mindful self- compassion intervention: A randomized control study. *Journal of Nervous and Mental Disease, 208*(2), 101–7.

Gutierrez-Galve, L., Stein, A., Hanington, L., Heron, J., & Ramchandani, P. (2015). Paternal depression in the postnatal period and child development: Mediators and moderators. *Pediatrics, 135*(2), e339–47.

Haga, S. M., Drozd, F., Lisøy, C., Wentzel-Larsen, T., & Slinning, K. (2019). Mamma Mia: A randomized controlled trial of an internet-based intervention for perinatal depression. *Psychological Medicine, 49*(11), 1850–58. https://doi.org/10.1017/S0033291718002544

Haines, B. A., Metalsky, G. I., Cardamone, A. L., & Joiner, T. (1999). Interpersonal and cognitive pathways into the origins of attributional style: A developmental perspective. In T. Joiner & J.C. Coyne (Eds.), *The interactional nature of depression: Advances in interpersonal approaches.* Washington, DC: American Psychological Association, pp. 65–92. https://doi.org/10.1037/10311-003

Halgunseth, L. C., Ispa, J. M., & Rudy, D. (2006). Parental control in Latino families: An integrated review of the literature. *Child Development, 77*(5), 1282–97.

Hamilton, J. L., & Alloy, L. B. (2016). Atypical reactivity of heart rate variability to stress and depression across development: Systematic review of the literature and directions for future research. *Clinical Psychology Review, 50*, 67–79. https://doi.org/10.1016/j.cpr.2016.09.003

Hammen, C. (2005). Stress and depression. *Annual Review of Clinical Psychology, 1*(1), 293–319. https://doi.org/10.1146/annurev.clinpsy.1.102803.143938

Hankin, B. L. (2017). Depression during childhood and adolescence. In R. J. DeRubeis & D. R. Strunk (Eds.), *The oxford handbook of mood disorders.* New York: Oxford University Press, pp. 276–86.

Hankin, B. L., & Abela, J. R. Z. (2005). Depression from childhood through adolescence and adulthood: A developmental vulnerability and stress perspective. In B. L. Hankin & J. R. Z. Abela (Eds.), *Development of psychopathology: A vulnerability-stress perspective.* Thousand Oaks, CA: Sage, pp. 245–88. https://doi.org/10.4135/9781452231655.n10

Hankin, B. L., Badanes, L. S., Abela, J. R., & Watamura, S. E. (2010). Hypothalamic–pituitary–adrenal axis dysregulation in dysphoric children and adolescents: Cortisol reactivity to psychosocial stress from preschool through middle adolescence. *Biological Psychiatry, 68*(5), 484–90.

Hankin, B. L., Davis, E. P., Snyder, H., Young, J. F., Glynn, L. M., & Sandman, C. A. (2017). Temperament factors and dimensional, latent bifactor models of child psychopathology: Transdiagnostic and specific associations in two youth samples. *Psychiatry Research, 252*, 139–46. https://doi.org/10.1016/j.psychres.2017.02.061

Hankin, B. L., Fraley, R. C., Lahey, B. B., & Waldman, I. D. (2005). Is depression best viewed as a continuum or discrete category? A taxometric analysis of childhood and adolescent depression in a population-based sample. *Journal of Abnormal Psychology, 114*(1), 96–110. https://doi.org/10.1037/0021-843X.114.1.96

Hankin, B. L., Lakdawalla, Z., Carter, I. L., Abela, J. R., & Adams, P. (2007). Are neuroticism, cognitive vulnerabilities and self–esteem overlapping or distinct risks for depression? Evidence from exploratory and confirmatory factor analyses. *Journal of Social and Clinical Psychology, 26*(1), 29–63.

Hankin, B. L., Oppenheimer, C., Jenness, J., Barrocas, A., Shapero, B. G., & Goldband, J. (2009). Developmental origins of cognitive vulnerabilities to depression: Review of processes contributing to stability and change across time. *Journal of Clinical Psychology, 65*(12), 1327–38. https://doi.org/10.1002/jclp.20625

Hankin, B. L., Snyder, H. R., & Gulley, L. D. (2016). Cognitive risks in developmental psychopathology. In D. Cicchetti (Ed.), *Developmental psychopathology: Maladaptation and psychopathology.* Hoboken, NJ: Wiley, pp. 312–385. https://doi.org/10.1002/9781119125556.devpsy308

Hannigan, L. J., Rijsdijk, F. V., Ganiban, J. M. et al. (2018). Shared genetic influences do not explain the association between parent–offspring relationship quality and offspring internalizing problems: Results from a Children-of-Twins study. *Psychological Medicine, 48*(4), 592–603. https://doi.org/10.1017/S0033291717001908

Harrington, R., Peters, S., Green, J., Byford, S., Woods, J., & McGowan, R. (2000). Randomized comparison of the effectiveness and costs of community and hospital based mental health services for children with behavioral disorders. *British Journal of Medicine, 321*(7268), 1–5.

Hartman, S., & Belsky, J. (2018). Prenatal programming of postnatal plasticity revisited: And extended. *Development and Psychopathology, 30*(3), 825–42. https://doi.org/10.1017/S0954579418000548

Hastings, P. D., Helm, J., Mills, R. S. L., Serbin, L. A., Stack, D. M., & Schwartzman, A. E. (2015). Dispositional and environmental predictors of the development of internalizing problems in childhood: Testing a multilevel model. *Journal of Abnormal Child Psychology, 43*(5), 831–45. https://doi.org /10.1007/s10802-014-9951-0

Hayden, E. P., Klein, D. N., Durbin, C. E., & Olino, T. M. (2006). Positive emotionality at age 3 predicts cognitive styles in 7-year-old children. *Development and Psychopathology, 18*(2), 409–23. https://doi.org/10.1017 /S0954579406060226

Hedges, L. V. & Olkin, I. (1985). *Statistical methods for meta-analysis.* Orlando, FL: Academic Press.

Hendrix, C. L., Stowe, Z. N., Newport, D. J., & Brennan, P. A. (2018). Physiological attunement in mother–infant dyads at clinical high risk: The influence of maternal depression and positive parenting. *Development and Psychopathology, 30*(2), 623–34.

Hochberg, Z., Feil, R., Constancia, M. et al. (2011). Child health, developmental plasticity, and epigenetic programming. *Endocrine Reviews, 32*(2), 159–224. https://doi.org/10.1210/er.2009-0039

Hoffman, C., Crnic, K. A., & Baker, J. K. (2006). Maternal depression and parenting: Implications for children's emergent emotion regulation and behavioral functioning. *Parenting: Science and Practice, 6*(4), 271–95. https://doi.org/10.1207/s15327922par0604_1

Hopkins, J., Lavigne, J. V., Gouze, K. R., LeBailly, S. A., & Bryant, F. B. (2013). Multi-domain models of risk factors for depression and anxiety symptoms in preschoolers: Evidence for common and specific factors. *Journal of Abnormal Child Psychology, 41*(5), 705–22.

Hughes, C., Roman, G., Hart, M. J., & Ensor, R. (2013). Does maternal depression predict young children's executive function? A 4-year longitudinal study. *Journal of Child Psychology and Psychiatry, 54*(2), 169–77. https://doi.org/10.1111/jcpp.12014

Huizink, A. C. (2008). Prenatal stress exposure and temperament: A review. *International Journal of Developmental Science, 2*(1–2), 77–99.

Hulvershorn, L. A., Cullen, K., & Anand, A. (2011). Toward dysfunctional connectivity: A review of neuroimaging findings in pediatric major depressive disorder. *Brain Imaging and Behavior, 5*(4), 307–28.

Ingoldsby, E. M., Kohl, G. O., McMahon, R. J., & Lengua, L. (2006). Conduct problems, depressive symptomatology and their co-occurring presentation in childhood as predictors of adjustment in early adolescence. *Journal of Abnormal Child Psychology, 34*(5), 603–21. https://doi.org/10.1007/s10802-006-9044-9

Ip, P., Li, T. M. H., Chan, K. L. et al. (2018). Associations of paternal postpartum depressive symptoms and infant development in a Chinese longitudinal study. *Infant Behavior and Development, 53*, 81–89. https://doi.org/10.1016/j.infbeh.2018.08.002

Jacob, T., & Johnson, S. L. (1997). Parent–child interaction among depressed fathers and mothers: Impact on child functioning. *Journal of Family Psychology, 11*(4), 391–409. https://doi.org/10.1037/0893-3200.11.4.391

Jacobs, R. H., Reinecke, M. A., Gollan, J. K., & Kane, P. (2008). Empirical evidence of cognitive vulnerability for depression among children and adolescents: A cognitive science and developmental perspective. *Clinical Psychology Review, 28*(5), 759–82.

Joinson, C., Kounali, D., & Lewis, G. (2017). Family socioeconomic position in early life and onset of depressive symptoms and depression: A prospective cohort study. *Social Psychiatry and Psychiatric Epidemiology, 52*(1), 95–103. https://doi.org/10.1007/s00127-016-1308-2.

Jones, E. J., Rohleder, N., & Schreier, H. M. (2020). Neuroendocrine coordination and youth behavior problems: A review of studies assessing sympathetic nervous system and hypothalamic-pituitary adrenal axis activity using salivary alpha amylase and salivary cortisol. *Hormones and Behavior, 122*, 104750.

Kane, P., & Garber, J. (2004). The relations among depression in fathers, children's psychopathology, and father-child conflict: A meta-analysis. *Clinical Psychology Review, 24*(3), 339–60. https://doi.org/10.1016/j.cpr.2004.03.004

Karnaze, M. M., & Levine, L. J. (2018). Sadness, the architect of cognitive change. In H. C. Lench (Ed.), *The function of emotions: When and why emotions help us.* New York: Springer, pp. 45–58. https://doi.org/10.1007/978-3-319-77619-4_4

Kaufman, J., Martin, A., King, R. A., & Charney, D. (2001). Are child-, adolescent-, and adult-onset depression one and the same disorder? *Biological Psychiatry, 49*(12), 980–1001.

Kemp, A. H., Quintana, D. S., Gray, M. A., Felmingham, K. L., Brown, K., & Gatt, J. M. (2010). Impact of depression and antidepressant treatment on heart rate variability: A review and meta-analysis. *Biological Psychiatry, 67*(11), 1067–74.

Keren, H., O'Callaghan, G., Vidal-Ribas, P. et al. (2018). Reward processing in depression: A conceptual and meta-analytic review across fMRI and EEG studies. *American Journal of Psychiatry, 175*(11), 1111–20.

Kiernan, K. E., & Huerta, M. C. (2008). Economic deprivation, maternal depression, parenting and children's cognitive and emotional development in early childhood. *British Journal of Sociology, 59*(4), 783–806. https://doi.org/10.1111/j.1468-4446.2008.00219.x

Kiff, C. J., Lengua, L. J., & Zalewski, M. (2011). Nature and nurturing: Parenting in the context of child temperament. *Clinical Child and Family Psychology Review, 14*(3), 251–301. https://doi.org/10.1007/s10567-011-0093-4

Kim, J., & Cicchetti, D. (2006). Longitudinal trajectories of self-system processes and depressive symptoms among maltreated and non-maltreated children. *Child Development, 77*(3), 624–39. https://doi.org/10.1111/j.1467-8624.2006.00894.x

Kistner, J., Balthazor, M., Risi, S., & Burton, C. (1999). Predicting dysphoria in adolescence from actual and perceived peer acceptance in childhood. *Journal of Clinical Child Psychology, 28*(1), 94–104. https://doi.org/10.1207/s15374424jccp2801_8

Kiviruusu, O., Pietikäinen, J. T., Kylliäinen, A. et al. (2020). Trajectories of mothers' and fathers' depressive symptoms from pregnancy to 24 months postpartum. *Journal of Affective Disorders, 260*, 629–37. https://doi.org/10.1016/j.jad.2019.09.038

Kochanska, G., Friesenborg, A. E., Lange, L. A., & Martel, M. M. (2004). Parents' personality and infants' temperament as contributors to their emerging relationship. *Journal of Personality and Social Psychology, 86*(5), 744–59. https://doi.org/10.1037/0022-3514.86.5.744

Kochel, K. P., Ladd, G. W., & Rudolph, K. D. (2012). Longitudinal associations among youth depressive symptoms, peer victimization, and low peer acceptance: An interpersonal process perspective. *Child Development, 83*(2), 637–50. https://doi.org/10.1111/j.1467-8624.2011.01722.x

Koenig, J., Kemp, A. H., Beauchaine, T. P., Thayer, J. F., & Kaess, M. (2016). Depression and resting state heart rate variability in children and adolescents: A systematic review and meta-analysis. *Clinical Psychology Review, 46*, 136–50. https://doi.org/10.1016/j.cpr.2016.04.013

Korja, R., Nolvi, S., Grant, K. A., & McMahon, C. (2017). The relations between maternal prenatal anxiety or stress and child's early negative reactivity or self-regulation: A systematic review. *Child Psychiatry and Human Development, 48*(6), 851–69. https://doi.org/10.1007/s10578-017-0709-0

Kotelnikova, Y., Mackrell, S. V. M., Jordan, P. L., & Hayden, E. P. (2015). Longitudinal associations between reactive and regulatory temperament traits and depressive symptoms in middle childhood. *Journal of Clinical Child and Adolescent Psychology, 44*(5), 775–86. https://doi.org/10.1080/15374416.2014.893517

Krygsman, A., & Vaillancourt, T. (2017). Longitudinal associations between depression symptoms and peer experiences: Evidence of symptoms-driven pathways. *Journal of Applied Developmental Psychology, 51*, 20–34. https://doi.org/10.1016/j.appdev.2017.05.003

Kuckertz, J. M., Mitchell, C., & Wiggins, J. L. (2018). Parenting mediates the impact of maternal depression on child internalizing symptoms. *Depression and Anxiety, 35*(1), 89–97. https://doi.org/10.1002/da.22688

Lahey, B. B., Loeber, R., Burke, J., Rathouz, P. J., & McBurnett, K. (2002). Waxing and waning in concert: Dynamic comorbidity of conduct disorder with other disruptive and emotional problems over 17 years among clinic-referred boys. *Journal of Abnormal Psychology 111*(4), 556–67.

Lakdawalla, Z., Hankin, B. L., & Mermelstein, R. (2007). Cognitive theories of depression in children and adolescents: A conceptual and quantitative review. *Clinical Child and Family Psychology Review, 10*(1), 1–24.

Lansford, J. E., Chang, L., Dodge, K. A. et al. (2005). Physical discipline and children's adjustment: Cultural normativeness as a moderator. *Child Development, 76*(6), 1234–46. https://doi.org/10.1111/j.1467-8624.2005.00847.x

Lee, E. W., Denison, F. C., Hor, K., & Reynolds, R. M. (2016). Web-based interventions for prevention and treatment of perinatal mood disorders: A systematic review. *BioMed Cental Pregnancy and Childbirth, 16*, 38. https://doi.org/10.1186/s12884-016-0831-1

Leech, S. L., Larkby, C. A., Day, R., & Day, N. L. (2006). Predictors and correlates of high levels of depression and anxiety symptoms among children at age 10. *Journal of the American Academy of Child and Adolescent Psychiatry, 45*(2), 223–30. https://do.org/10.1097/01.ch.0000184930.18552.4d

Lemery, K. S., Essex, M. J., & Smider, N. A. (2002). Revealing the relation between temperament and behavior problem symptoms by eliminating measurement confounding: Expert ratings and factor analyses. *Child Development, 73*(3), 867–82. https://doi.org/10.1111/1467-8624.00444

LeMoult, J., Humphreys, K. L., Tracy, A., Hoffmeister, J. A., Ip, E., & Gotlib, I. H. (2020). Meta-analysis: Exposure to early life stress and risk for depression in childhood and adolescence. *Journal of the American Academy of Child and Adolescent Psychiatry, 59*(7), 842–55. https://doi.org/10.1016/j.jaac.2019.10.011

Lengua, L. J., & Long, A. C. (2002). The role of emotionality and self-regulation in the appraisal–coping process: Tests of direct and moderating effects. *Journal of Applied Developmental Psychology, 23*(4), 471–93.

Leppert, K. A., Bufferd, S. J., Olino, T. M., & Dougherty, L. R. (2019). A daily diary analysis of preschool depressive behaviors: Prospective associations and moderators across 14 days. *Journal of Abnormal Child Psychology, 47* (9), 1547–58. https://doi.org/10.1007/s10802-019-00535-4

Lewinsohn, P. M., Steinmetz, J. L., Larson, D. W., & Franklin, J. (1981). Depression-related cognitions: Antecedent or consequence? *Journal of Abnormal Psychology, 90*(3), 213–19. https://doi.org/10.1037//0021-843x .90.3.213

Lewis, A. J., & Olsson, C. A. (2011). Early life stress and child temperament style as predictors of childhood anxiety and depressive symptoms: Findings from the longitudinal study of Australian children. *Depression Research and Treatment,* 2011, 296026. https://doi.org/10.1155/2011/296026

Lewis, J. H., Sae-Koew, A. J., Toumbourou, J. W., & Bosco, R. (2020). Gender differences in trajectories of depressive symptoms across childhood and adolescence: A multi-group growth mixture model. *Journal of Affective Disorders, 260,* 463–72.

Lin, B., Crnic, K., Luecken, L. J., & Gonzales, N. (2017). Ontogeny of emotional and behavioral problems in a low-income, Mexican American sample. *Developmental Psychology, 53*(12), 2245–60. https://doi.org/10 .1037/dev0000391

Lin, B., Yeo, A. J., Luecken, L. J., & Roubinov, D. S. (2020). Effects of maternal and paternal postnatal depressive symptoms on infants' parasympathetic regulation in low-income, Mexican American families. *Developmental Psychobiology.* Advance online publication. https://doi.org/10.1002/dev .22073

Lin, B, Kidwell, M. C., Kerig, P. K., Crowell, S. E., & Fortuna, A. J. (2021). Profiles of autonomic stress responsivity in a sample of justice-involved youth: Associations with childhood trauma exposure and emotional and behavioral functioning. *Developmental Psychobiology, 63*(2), 206–25. https://doi.org/10.1002/dev.21968

Lopez-Duran, N. L., Kovacs, M., & George, C. J. (2009). Hypothalamic–pituitary–adrenal axis dysregulation in depressed children and adolescents: A meta-analysis. *Psychoneuroendocrinology, 34*(9), 1272–83. https://doi.org /10.1016/j.psyneuen.2009.03.016

Lopez-Duran, N. L., McGinnis, E., Kuhlman, K., Geiss, E., Vargas, I., & Mayer, S. (2015). HPA-axis stress reactivity in youth depression: Evidence of impaired regulatory processes in depressed boys. *Stress, 18*(5), 545–53. https://doi.org/10.3109/10253890.2015.1053455

Lovejoy, M. C., Graczyk, P. A., O'Hare, E., & Neuman, G. (2000). Maternal depression and parenting behavior: A meta-analytic review. *Clinical*

Psychology Review, 20(5), 561–92. https://doi.org/10.1016/S0272-7358(98)00100-7

Luby, J. L., Barch, D. M., Whalen, D., Tillman, R., & Freedland, K. E. (2018). A randomized controlled trial of parent-child psychotherapy targeting emotion development for early childhood depression. *American Journal of Psychiatry, 175*(11), 1102–10. https://doi.org/10.1176/appi.ajp.2018.18030321

Luby, J. L., Belden, A., Sullivan, J., & Spitznagel, E. (2007). Preschoolers' contribution to their diagnosis of depression and anxiety: Uses and limitations of young child self-report of symptoms. *Child Psychiatry and Human Development, 38*(4), 321–38. https://doi.org/10.1007/s10578-007-0063-8

Luby, J. L., Belden, A. C., Pautsch, J., Si, X., & Spitznagel, E. (2009a). The clinical significance of preschool depression: Impairment in functioning and clinical markers of the disorder. *Journal of Affective Disorders, 112*(1–3), 111–19. https://doi.org/10.1016/j.jad.2008.03.026

Luby, J., Belden, A., Sullivan, J., Hayen, R., McCadney, A., & Spitznagel, E. (2009b). Shame and guilt in preschool depression: Evidence for elevations in self-conscious emotions in depression as early as age 3. *Journal of Child Psychology and Psychiatry, 50*(9), 1156–66. https://doi.org/10.1111/j.1469-7610.2009.02077.x

Luby, J. L., Si, X., Belden, A. C., Tandon, M., & Spitznagel, E. (2009c). Preschool depression: Homotypic continuity and course over 24 months. *Archives of General Psychiatry, 66*(8), 897–905. https://doi.org/10.1001/archgenpsychiatry.2009.97

Luby, J. L., Gaffrey, M. S., Tillman, R., April, L. M., & Belden, A. C. (2014). Trajectories of preschool disorders to full DSM depression at school age and early adolescence: Continuity of preschool depression. *American Journal of Psychiatry, 171*(7), 768–76. https://doi.org/10.1176/appi.ajp.2014.13091198

Luby, J. L., Heffelfinger, A. K., Mrakotsky, C., Hessler, M. J., Brown, K. M., & Hildebrand, T. (2002). Preschool major depressive disorder: Preliminary validation for developmentally modified criteria. *Journal of the American Academy of Child and Adolescent Psychiatry, 41*(8), 928–37. https://doi.org/10.1097/00004583-200208000-00011

Luby, J. L., Heffelfinger, A., Mrakotsky, C., Brown, K., Hessler, M., & Spitznagel, E. (2003). Alterations in stress cortisol reactivity in depressed preschoolers relative to psychiatric and no-disorder comparison groups. *Archives of General Psychiatry, 60*(12), 1248–55.

Luebbe, A. M., & Bell, D. J. (2014). Positive and negative family emotional climate differentially predict youth anxiety and depression via distinct affective Pathways. *Journal of Abnormal Child Psychology*, *42*(6), 897–911. https://doi.org/10.1007/s10802-013-9838-5

Luking, K. R., Pagliaccio, D., Luby, J. L., & Barch, D. M. (2016). Reward processing and risk for depression across development. *Trends in Cognitive Sciences*, *20*(6), 456–68. https://doi.org/10.1016/j.tics.2016.04.002

Manian, N., & Bornstein, M. H. (2009). Dynamics of emotion regulation in infants of clinically depressed and nondepressed mothers. *Journal of Child Psychology and Psychiatry*, *50*(11), 1410–18. https://doi.org/10.1111/j.1469-7610.2009.02166.x

Mäntymaa, M., Puura, K., Luoma, I., Salmelin, R. K., & Tamminen, T. (2006). Mother's early perception of her infant's difficult temperament, parenting stress and early mother–infant interaction. *Nordic Journal of Psychiatry*, *60*(5), 379–86. https://doi.org/10.1080/08039480600937280

Maughan, B., Collishaw, S., & Stringaris, A. (2013). Depression in childhood and adolescence. *Journal of the Canadian Academy of Child and Adolescent Psychiatry*, *22*(1), 35–40.

McDaniel, B. T., & Radesky, J. S. (2018). Technoference: Parent distraction with technology and associations with child behavior problems. *Child Development*, *89*(1), 100–9. https://doi.org/10.1111/cdev.12822

McDonough-Caplan, H., Klein, D. N., & Beauchaine, T. P. (2018). Comorbidity and continuity of depression and conduct problems from elementary school to adolescence. *Journal of Abnormal Psychology*, *127*(3), 326–37. https://doi.org/10.1037/abn0000339

McElroy, E., Fearon, P., Belsky, J., Fonagy, P., & Patalay, P. (2018). Networks of depression and anxiety symptoms across development. *Journal of the American Academy of Child and Adolescent Psychiatry*, *57*(12), 964–73. https://doi.org/10.1016/j.jaac.2018.05.027

McElwain, N. L., & Volling, B. L. (1999). Depressed mood and marital conflict: Relations to maternal and paternal intrusiveness with one-year-old infants. *Journal of Applied Developmental Psychology*, *20*(1), 63–83.

McGee, R., & Williams, S. (1988). Childhood depression and reading ability: Is there a relationship? *Journal of School Psychology*, *26*(4), 391–94.

McLaughlin, K. A. (2016). Future directions in childhood adversity and youth psychopathology. *Journal of Clinical Child and Adolescent Psychology*, *45*(3), 361–82. https://doi.org/10.1080/15374416.2015.1110823

McLaughlin, K. A., & Sheridan, M. A. (2016). Beyond cumulative risk: A dimensional approach to childhood adversity. *Current Directions in Psychological Science*, *25*(4), 239–45.

Melton, T. H., Croarkin, P. E., Strawn, J. R., & Mcclintock, S. M. (2016). Comorbid anxiety and depressive symptoms in children and adolescents:

A systematic review and analysis. *Journal of Psychiatric Practice, 22*(2), 84–98. https://doi.org/10.1097/PRA.0000000000000132

Mesman, J., van Ijzendoorn, M. H., & Bakermans-Kranenburg, M. J. (2009). The many faces of the Still-Face Paradigm: A review and meta-analysis. *Developmental Review, 29*(2), 120–62. https://doi.org/10.1016/j.dr.2009.02.001

Mezulis, A. H., Hyde, J. S., & Abramson, L. Y. (2006). The developmental origins of cognitive vulnerability to depression: Temperament, parenting, and negative life events in childhood as contributors to negative cognitive style. *Developmental Psychology, 42*(6), 1012–25. https://doi.org/10.1037/0012-1649.42.6.1012

Micco, J. A., Henin, A., Biederman, J. et al. (2009). Executive functioning in offspring at risk for depression and anxiety. *Depression and Anxiety, 26*(9), 780–90. https://doi.org/10.1002/da.2057

Mlawer, F., Hubbard, J. A., Bookhout, M. K. et al. (2019). Bidirectional relations between internalizing symptoms and peer victimization in late childhood. *Social Development, 28*(4), 942–59.

Monroe, S. M., & Simons, A. D. (1991). Diathesis-stress theories in the context of life stress research: Implications for the depressive disorders. *Psychological Bulletin, 110*(3), 406–25.

Moran, K. M., Root, A. E., Vizy, B. K., Wilson, T. K., & Gentzler, A. L. (2019). Maternal socialization of children's positive affect regulation: Associations with children's savoring, dampening, and depressive symptoms. *Social Development, 28*(2), 306–22. https://doi.org/10.1111/sode.12338

Morelen, D., Shaffer, A., & Suveg, C. (2016). Maternal emotion regulation: Links to emotion parenting and child emotion regulation. *Journal of Family Issues, 37*(13), 1891–1916.

Morris, A. S., Silk, J. S., Steinberg, L., Myers, S. S., & Robinson, L. R. (2007). The role of the family context in the development of emotion regulation. *Social Development, 16*(2), 361–88. https://doi.org/10.1111/j.1467-9507.2007.00389.x

Murray, L., Hipwell, A., Hooper, R., Stein, A., & Cooper, P. (1996). The cognitive development of 5-year-old children of postnatally depressed mothers. *The Journal of Child Psychology and Psychiatry and Allied Disciplines, 37*(8), 927–35. https://doi.org/10.1111/j.1469-7610.1996.tb01490.x

Murray, L., Marwick, H., & Arteche, A. (2010). Sadness in mothers' "baby-talk" predicts affective disorder in adolescent offspring. *Infant Behavior and Development, 33*(3), 361–64. https://doi.org/10.1016/j.infbeh.2010.03.009

Natsuaki, M. N., Shaw, D. S., Neiderhiser, J. M. et al. (2014). Raised by depressed parents: Is it an environmental risk? *Clinical Child and Family*

Psychology Review, 17(4), 357–67. https://doi.org/10.1007/s10567-014-0169-z

Nearchou, F., Flinn, C., Niland, R., Subramanium, S.S, & Hennessy, E. (2020). Exploring the impact of Covid-19 on mental health outcomes of children and adolescents: *A systematic review. International Journal of Environmental Review and Public Health, 17*(22), 8479. https://doi.org/10.3390/ijerph17228479

Neiss, M. B., Stevenson, J., Legrand, L. N., Iacono, W. G., & Sedikides, C. (2009). Self-esteem, negative emotionality, and depression as a common temperamental core: A study of mid-adolescent twin girls. *Journal of Personality, 77*(2), 327–46. https://doi.org/10.1111/j.1467-6494.2008.00549.x

Newland, R. P., Ciciolla, L., & Crnic, K. A. (2015). Crossover effects among parental hostility and parent–child relationships during the preschool period. *Journal of Child and Family Studies, 24*(7), 2107–19.

Nigg, J. T. (2006). Temperament and developmental psychopathology. *Journal of Child Psychology and Psychiatry, 47*(3–4), 395–422. https://doi.org/10.1111/j.1469-7610.2006.01612.x

Nolen-Hoeksema, S. (2004). The response styles theory. In C. Papageorgiou & A. Wells (Eds.), *Depressive rumination: Nature, theory and treatment.* Chichester: Wiley, pp. 107–23.

Nolen-Hoeksema, S., & Watkins, E. R. (2011). A heuristic for developing transdiagnostic models of psychopathology: Explaining multifinality and divergent trajectories. *Perspectives on Psychological Science, 6*(6), 589–609.

Norcross, P. L., Bailes, L. G., & Leerkes, E. (2020). Effects of maternal depressive symptoms on sensitivity to infant distress and non-distress: Role of SES and race. *Infant Behavior and Development, 61*, 6. https://doi.org/10.1016/jinfbeh.2020.101498

O'Connor, E. E., Langer, D. A., & Tompson, M. C. (2017). Maternal depression and youth internalizing and externalizing symptomatology: Severity and chronicity of past maternal depression and current maternal depressive symptoms. *Journal of Abnormal Child Psychology, 45*(3), 557–68. https://doi.org/10.1007/s10802-016-0185-1

O'Donnell, K. J., Jensen, A. B., Freeman, L., Khalife, N., O'Connor, T. G., & Glover, V. (2012). Maternal prenatal anxiety and downregulation of placental 11β-HSD2. *Psychoneuroendocrinology, 37*(6), 818–26.

O'Donnell, K. J., & Meaney, M. J. (2017). Fetal origins of mental health: The developmental origins of health and disease hypothesis. *American Journal of Psychiatry, 174*(4), 319–28. https://doi.org/10.1176/appi.ajp.2016.16020138

Oldehinkel, A. J., Veenstra, R., Ormel, J., De Winter, A. F., & Verhulst, F. C. (2006). Temperament, parenting, and depressive symptoms in a population sample of preadolescents. *Journal of Child Psychology and Psychiatry, 47* (7), 684–95. https://doi.org/10.1111/j.1469-7610.2005.01535.x

Olweus, D., & Limber, S. P. (2018). Some problems with cyberbullying research. *Current Opinion in Psychology, 19*, 139–43. https://doi.org/10.1016/j.copsyc.2017.04.012

Pang, K. C., & Beauchaine, T. P. (2013). Longitudinal patterns of autonomic nervous system responding to emotion evocation among children with conduct problems and/or depression. *Developmental Psychobiology, 55*(7), 698–706.

Pariante, C. M., & Lightman, S. L. (2008). The HPA axis in major depression: Classical theories and new developments. *Trends in Neurosciences, 31*(9), 464–68.

Paulson, J. F., & Bazemore, S. D. (2010). Prenatal and postpartum depression in fathers and its association with maternal depression: A meta-analysis. *Journal of the American Medical Association, 303*(19), 1961–69. https://doi.org/10.1001/jama.2010.605

Pearson, R. M., Bornstein, M. H., Cordero, M. et al. (2016). Maternal perinatal mental health and offspring academic achievement at age 16: The mediating role of childhood executive function. *Journal of Child Psychology and Psychiatry, 57*(4), 491–501. https://doi.org/10.1111/jcpp.12483

Piteo, A. M., Yelland, L. N., & Makrides, M. (2012). Does maternal depression predict developmental outcome in 18 month old infants? *Early Human Development, 88*(8), 651–55. https://doi.org/10.1016/j.earlhumdev.2012.01.013

Pitzer, M., Esser, G., Schmidt, M. H., Hohm, E., Banaschewski, T., & Laucht, M. (2017). Child regulative temperament as a mediator of parenting in the development of depressive symptoms: A longitudinal study from early childhood to preadolescence. *Journal of Neural Transmission, 124*(5), 631–41. https://doi.org/10.1007/s00702-017-1682-2

Pluess, M., & Belsky, J. (2011). Prenatal programming of postnatal plasticity? *Development and Psychopathology, 23*(1), 29–38. https://doi.org/10.1017/s0954579410000623

Porges, S. W. (2007). The polyvagal perspective. *Biological Psychology, 74*(2), 116–43. https://doi.org/10.1016/j.biopsycho.2006.06.009

Priel, A., Djalovski, A., Zagoory-Sharon, O., & Feldman, R. (2019). Maternal depression impacts child psychopathology across the first decade of life: Oxytocin and synchrony as markers of resilience. *Journal of Child Psychology and Psychiatry, 60*(1), 30–42. https://doi.org/10.1111/jcpp.12880

Priel, A., Zeev-Wolf, M., Djalovski, A., & Feldman, R. (2020). Maternal depression impairs child emotion understanding and executive functions:

The role of dysregulated maternal care across the first decade of life. *Emotion*, *20*(6), 1042–58. https://doi.org/10.1037/emo0000614

Priest, N., Paradies, Y., Trenerry, B., Truong, M., Karlsen, S., & Kelly, Y. (2013). A systematic review of studies examining the relationship between reported racism and health and wellbeing for children and young people. *Social Science and Medicine*, *95*, 115–27.

Prinstein, M. J., Cheah, C. S. L., & Guyer, A. E. (2005). Peer victimization, cue interpretation, and internalizing symptoms: Preliminary concurrent and longitudinal findings for children and adolescents. *Journal of Clinical Child and Adolescent Psychology*, *34*(1), 11–24. https://doi.org/10.1207 /s15374424jccp3401_2

Putnam, S. P., Gartstein, M. A., & Rothbart, M. K. (2006). Measurement of fine-grained aspects of toddler temperament: The Early Childhood Behavior Questionnaire. *Infant Behavior and Development*, *29*(3), 386–401. https://doi .org/10.1016/j.infbeh.2006.01.004

Putnick, D. L., Sundaram, R., Bell, E. M. et al. (2020). Trajectories of maternal postpartum depressive symptoms. *Pediatrics*, *146*(5), e20200857. https://doi .org/10.1542/peds.2020-085

Ramchandani, P., Stein, A., Evans, J., & O'Connor, T. G. (2005). Paternal depression in the postnatal period and child development: A prospective population study. *The Lancet*, *365*(9478), 2201–5. https://doi.org/10.1016 /S0140-6736(05)66778-5

Rao, U. & Chen, L. A. (2009). Characteristics, correlates, and outcomes of childhood and adolescent depressive disorders. *Dialogues in Clinical Neuroscience*, *11*(1), 45–62.

Rao, U., Hammen, C., Ortiz, L. R., Chen, L. A., & Poland, R. E. (2008). Effects of early and recent adverse experiences on adrenal response to psychosocial stress in depressed adolescents. *Biological Psychiatry*, *64*(6), 521–26.

Reijntjes, A., Kamphuis, J. H., Prinzie, P., & Telch, M. J. (2010). Peer victimization and internalizing problems in children: A meta-analysis of longitudinal studies. *Child Abuse and Neglect*, *34*(4), 244–52. https://doi.org/10 .1016/j.chiabu.2009.07.009

Reinfjell, T., Kårstad, S. B., Berg-Nielsen, T. S., Luby, J. L., & Wichstrøm, L. (2016). Predictors of change in depressive symptoms from preschool to first grade. *Development and Psychopathology*, *28*(4pt2), 1517–30. https://doi .org/10.1017/S0954579415001170

Rhoades, B. L., Greenberg, M. T., Lanza, S. T., & Blair, C. (2011). Demographic and familial predictors of early executive function development: Contribution of a person-centered perspective. *Journal of Experimental Child Psychology*, *108*(3), 638–62. https://doi.org/10.1016/j.jecp.2010.08.004

Rice, F. (2010). Genetics of childhood and adolescent depression: Insights into etiological heterogeneity and challenges for future genomic research. *Genome Medicine, 2*(9), 68. https://doi.org/10.1186/gm189

Rice, F., Harold, G., & Thapar, A. (2002). The genetic aetiology of childhood depression: A review. *Journal of Child Psychology and Psychiatry, 43*(1), 65–79. https://doi.org/10.1111/1469-7610.00004

Rooney, R., Hassan, S., Kane, R., Roberts, C. M., & Nesa, M. (2013). Reducing depression in 9–10 year old children in low SES schools: A longitudinal universal randomized controlled trial. *Behaviour Research and Therapy, 51* (12), 845–54. https://doi.org/10.1016/j.brat.2013.09.005

Rothbart, M. K. (2011). *Becoming who we are: Temperament and personality in development.* New York: Guilford Press.

Rothbart, M. K., Ahadi, S. A., Hershey, K. L., & Fisher, P. (2001). Investigations of temperament at three to seven years: The Children's Behavior Questionnaire. *Child Development, 72*(5), 1394–1408.

Rubin, K. H., & Coplan, R. J. (2007). Paying attention to and not neglecting social withdrawal and social isolation. In G. W. Ladd (Ed.), *Landscapes of childhood. Appraising the human developmental sciences: Essays in honor of Merrill-Palmer Quarterly.* Detroit, MI: Wayne State University Press, pp. 156–85.

Rudolph, K. D. (2009). The interpersonal context of adolescent depression. In S. Nolen-Hoeksema & L. M. Hilt (Eds.), *Handbook of depression in adolescents.* New York: Routledge, pp. 377–418.

Rudolph, K. D., Flynn, M., & Abaied, J. L. (2008). A developmental perspective on interpersonal theories of youth depression. In J. R. Z. Abela & B. L. Hankin (Eds.), *Child and adolescent depression: Cause, treatment, and prevention.* New York: Guilford Press, pp. 79–102.

Rudolph, K. D., Troop-Gordon, W., & Flynn, M. (2009). Relational victimization predicts children's social-cognitive and self-regulatory responses in a challenging peer context. *Developmental Psychology, 45*(5), 1444–54. https://doi.org/10.1037/0033-2909.112.3.461

Rudolph, K. D., Troop-Gordon, W., Hessel, E. T., & Schmidt, J. D. (2011). A latent growth curve analysis of early and increasing peer victimization as predictors of mental health across elementary school. *Journal of Clinical Child and Adolescent Psychology, 40*(1), 111–22. https://doi.org/10.1080/15374416.2011.533413

Ruscio, J., & Ruscio, A. M. (2000). Informing the continuity controversy: A taxometric analysis of depression. *Journal of Abnormal Psychology, 109* (3), 473–87. https://doi.org/10.1037/0021-843X.109.3.473

Sallquist, J., Eisenberg, N., French, D. C., Purwono, U., & Suryanti, T. A. (2010). Indonesian adolescents' spiritual and religious experiences and their longitudinal relations with socioemotional functioning. *Developmental Psychology, 46*(3), 699–716. https://doi.org/10.1037/a0018879

Sameroff, A. J. (1983). *Developmental systems: Contexts and evolution*, Vol. 1. New York: Wiley.

SAMHSA (Substance Abuse and Mental Health Services Administration). (2016). DSM-5 changes: Implications for child serious emotional disturbance. SAMHSA. https://www.samhsa.gov/data/sites/default/files/NSDUH-DSM5ImpactAdultMI-2016.pdf

Sander, L. W., Julia, H. L., Stechler, G., & Burns, P. (1972). Continuous 24-hour interactional monitoring in infants reared in two caretaking environments. *Psychosomatic Medicine, 34*(3), 270–82.

Sandman, C. A., Glynn, L. M., & Davis, E. P. (2013). Is there a viability-vulnerability tradeoff? Sex differences in fetal programming. *Journal of Psychosomatic Research, 75*(4), 327–35.

Scaramella, L. V., & Leve, L. D. (2004). Clarifying parent–child reciprocities during early childhood: The early childhood coercion model. *Clinical Child and Family Psychology Review, 7*(2), 89–107. https://doi.org/10.1023/B:CCFP.0000030287.13160.a3

Schlotz, W., & Phillips, D. I. W. (2009). Fetal origins of mental health: Evidence and mechanisms. *Brain, Behavior, and Immunity, 23*(7), 905–16. https://doi.org/10.1016/j.bbi.2009.02.001

Scorza, P., Duarte, C. S., Hipwell, A. E. et al. (2018). Research review: Intergenerational transmission of disadvantage: epigenetics and parents' childhoods as the first exposure. *Journal of Child Psychology and Psychiatry, 60*(2), 119–32. https://doi.org/10.1111/jcpp.12877

Seaton, E. K., Gee, G. C., Neblett, E., & Spanierman, L. (2018). New directions for racial discrimination research as inspired by the integrative model. *American Psychologist, 73*(6), 768–80.

Sethna, V., Murray, L., Edmondson, O., Iles, J., & Ramchandani, P. G. (2018). Depression and playfulness in fathers and young infants: A matched design comparison study. *Journal of Affective Disorders, 229*, 364–70.

Sethna, V., Murray, L., Netsi, E., Psychogiou, L., & Goodman, P. G. (2015). Paternal depression in the postnatal period and early father–infant interactions. *Parenting, 15*(1), 1–8.

Shannon, K. E., Beauchaine, T. P., Brenner, S. L., Neuhaus, E., & Gatzke-Kopp, L. (2007). Familial and temperamental predictors of resilience in children at risk for conduct disorder and depression. *Development and Psychopathology, 19*(3), 701–27. https://doi.org/10.1017/S0954579407000351

Shiner, R. L., Masten, A. S., & Tellegen, A. (2002). A developmental perspective on personality in emerging adulthood: Childhood antecedents and concurrent adaptation. *Journal of Personality and Social Psychology, 83*(5), 1165–77. https://doi.org/10.1037/0022-3514.83.5.1165

Shulman, B., Dueck, R., Ryan, D., Breau, G., Sadowski, I., & Misri, S. (2018). Feasibility of a mindfulness-based cognitive therapy group intervention as an adjunctive treatment for postpartum depression and anxiety. *Journal of Affective Disorders*, 235, 61–67. https://doi.org/10.1016/j.jad.2017.12.065

Silk, J. S., Shaw, D. S., Skuban, E. M., Oland, A. A., & Kovacs, M. (2006). Emotion regulation strategies in offspring of childhood-onset depressed mothers. *Journal of Child Psychology and Psychiatry, 47*(1), 69–78. https://doi.org/10.1111/j.1469-7610.2005.01440.x

Slagt, M., Dubas, J. S., Deković, M., & van Aken, M. A. G. (2016). Differences in sensitivity to parenting depending on child temperament: A meta-analysis. *Psychological Bulletin, 142*(10), 1068–1110. https://doi.org/10.1037/bul0000061

Snyder, H. R. (2013). Major depressive disorder is associated with broad impairments on neuropsychological measures of executive function: A meta-analysis and review. *Psychological Bulletin, 139*(1), 81–132. https://doi.org/10.1037/a0028727

Spry, E. A., Aarsman, S. R., Youssef, G. J. et al. (2020). Maternal and paternal depression and anxiety and offspring negative affectivity: A systematic review and meta-analysis. *Developmental Review*, 58, 19. https://doi.org/10.1016/j.dr.2020.100934

Sravish, A. V., Tronick, E., Hollenstein, T., & Beeghly, M. (2013). Dyadic flexibility during the face-to-face still-face paradigm: A dynamic systems analysis of its temporal organization. *Infant Behavior and Development, 36*(3), 432–37.

Stein, A., Pearson, R. M., Goodman, S. H. et al. (2014). Effects of perinatal mental disorders on the fetus and child. *The Lancet, 384*(9956), 1800–19. https://doi.org/10.1016/S0140-6736(14)61277-0

Stephens-Davidowitz, S. (2014). The cost of racial animus on a black candidate: Evidence using Google search data. *Journal of Public Economics, 118*, 26–40. https://doi.org/10.1016/j.jpubeco.2014.04.010

Stetler, C., & Miller, G. E. (2011). Depression and hypothalamic-pituitary-adrenal activation: A quantitative summary of four decades of research. *Psychosomatic Medicine, 73*(2), 114–26.

Stockdale, L. A., Porter, C. L., Coyne, S. M. et al. (2020). Infants' response to a mobile phone modified still-face paradigm: Links to maternal behaviors and beliefs regarding technoference. *Infancy, 25*(5), 571–92. https://doi.org/10.1111/infa.12342

Super, C. M., Axia, G., Harkness, S. et al. (2008). Culture, temperament, and the "difficult child": A study of seven Western cultures. *European Journal of Developmental Science, 2*(1–2), 136–57.

Sutter-Dallay, A., Murray, L., Dequae-Merchadou, L., Glatigny-Dallay, E., Bourgeois, M., & Verdoux, H. (2011). A prospective longitudinal study of the impact of early postnatal vs. chronic maternal depressive symptoms on child development. *European Psychiatry, 26*(8), 484–89. https://doi.org/10.1016/j.eurpsy.2010.05.004

Suzuki, H., Belden, A. C., Spitznagel, E., Dietrich, R., & Luby, J. L. (2013). Blunted stress cortisol reactivity and failure to acclimate to familiar stress in depressed and sub-syndromal children. *Psychiatry Research, 210*(2), 575–83. https://doi.org/10.1016/j.psychres.2013.06.038

Sweeney, S., & MacBeth, A. (2016). The effects of paternal depression on child and adolescent outcomes: A systematic review. *Journal of Affective Disorders, 205*, 44–59.

Taraban, L., Shaw, D. S., Leve, L. D. et al. (2017). Maternal depression and parenting in early childhood: Contextual influence of marital quality and social support in two samples. *Developmental Psychology, 53*(3), 436–49. https://doi.org/10.1037/dev0000261

Thapar, A., & Rice, F. (2006). Twin studies in pediatric depression. *Child and Adolescent Psychiatric Clinics of North America, 15*(4), 869–81. https://doi.org/10.1016/j.chc.2006.05.007

Tissot, H., Favez, N., Ghisletta, P., Frascarolo, F., & Despland, J.-N. (2017). A longitudinal study of parental depressive symptoms and coparenting in the first 18 months. *Family Process, 56*(2), 445–58. https://doi.org/10.1111/famp12213

Toenders, Y. J., van Velzen, L. S., Heideman, I. Z., Harrison, B. J., Davey, C. G., & Schmaal, L. (2019). Neuroimaging predictors of onset and course of depression in childhood and adolescence: A systematic review of longitudinal studies. *Developmental Cognitive Neuroscience, 39*, 100700. https://doi.org/10.1016/j.dcn.2019.100700

Tompson, M. C., Sugar, C. A., Langer, D. A., & Asarnow, J. R. (2017). A randomized clinical trial comparing family-focused treatment and individual supportive therapy for depression in childhood and early adolescence. *Journal of the American Academy of Child and Adolescent Psychiatry, 56*(6), 515–23. https://doi.org/10.1016/j.jaac.2017.03.018

Tram, J. M., & Cole, D. A. (2006). A multimethod examination of the stability of depressive symptoms in childhood and adolescence. *Journal of Abnormal Psychology, 115*(4), 674–86. https://doi.org/10.1037/0021-843X.115.4.674

Tronick, E. Z. (2007). *The neurobehavioral and social-emotional development of infants and children.* New York: Norton.

Tronick, E., Als, H., Adamson, L., Wise, S., & Brazelton, T. B. (1978). The infant's response to entrapment between contradictory messages in face-to-face interaction. *Journal of the American Academy of Child Psychiatry, 17* (1), 1–13.

Tronick, E. Z., & Reck, C. (2009). Infants of depressed mothers. *Harvard Review of Psychiatry, 17*(2), 147–56. https://doi.org/10.1080 /10673220902899714

Troop-Gordon, W., Rudolph, K. D., Sugimura, N., & Little, T. D. (2015). Peer victimization in middle childhood impedes adaptive responses to stress: A pathway to depressive symptoms. *Journal of Clinical Child and Adolescent Psychology, 44*(3), 432–45. https://doi.org/10.1080/15374416 .2014.891225

Tse, A. C., Rich-Edwards, J. W., Rifas-Shiman, S. L., Gillman, M. W., & Oken, E. (2010). Association of maternal prenatal depressive symptoms with child cognition at age 3 years. *Paediatric Perinatal Epidemiology, 24,* 232–40.

Turney, K. (2012). Prevalence and correlates of stability and change in maternal depression: Evidence from the fragile families and child wellbeing study. *PLoS One, 7*(9). https://doi.org/10.1371/journal.pone.0045709

Twenge, J. M., & Nolen-Hoeksema, S. (2002). Age, gender, race, socioeconomic status, and birth cohort difference on the children's depression inventory: A meta-analysis. *Journal of Abnormal Psychology, 111*(4), 578–88. https://doi.org/10.1037/0021-843X.111.4.578

Ulrich-Lai, Y. M., & Herman, J. P. (2009). Neural regulation of endocrine and autonomic stress responses. *Nature Reviews Neuroscience, 10*(6), 397–409. https://doi.org/10.1038/nrn2647

Valiente, C., Fabes, R. A., Eisenberg, N., & Spinrad, T. L. (2004). The relations of parental expressivity and support to children's coping with daily stress. *Journal of Family Psychology, 18*(1), 97–106. https://doi.org/10.1037/0893-3200.18.1.97

Vallotton, C., Harewood, T., Froyen, L., Brophy-Herb, H., & Ayoub, C. (2016). Child behavior problems: Mothers' and fathers' mental health matters today and tomorrow. *Early Childhood Research Quarterly, 37,* 81–93. https://doi .org/10.1016/j.ecresq.2016.02.006

Van Beveren, M. L., Mezulis, A., Wante, L., & Braet, C. (2019). Joint contributions of negative emotionality, positive emotionality, and effortful control on depressive symptoms in youth. *Journal of Clinical Child and Adolescent Psychology, 48*(1), 131–42. https://doi.org/10.1080/15374416 .2016.1233499

Van den Bergh, B. R. H., van den Heuvel, M. I., Lahti, M. et al. (2017). Prenatal developmental origins of behavior and mental health: The influence of maternal stress in pregnancy. *Neuroscience and Biobehavioral Reviews*, *117*, 26–64. https://doi.org/10.1016/j.neubiorev.2017.07.003

Van der Waerden, J., Galéra, C., Larroque, B., Saurel-Cubizolles, M., Sutter-Dallay, A., & Melchior, M. (2015). Maternal depression trajectories and children's behavior at age 5 years. *The Journal of Pediatrics*, *166*(6), 1440–48. https://doi.org/10.1016/j.jpeds.2015.03.002

Vidal-Ribas, P., Benson, B., Vitale, A. D. et al. (2019). Bidirectional association between stress and reward processing in children and adolescents: A longitudinal neuroimaging study. *Biological Psychiatry: Cognitive Neuroscience and Neuroimaging*, *4* (10), 893–901. https://doi.org/10.1016/j.bpsc.2019.05.012

Vilgis, V., Silk, T. J., & Vance, A. (2015). Executive function and attention in children and adolescents with depressive disorders: A systematic review. *European Child and Adolescent Psychiatry*, *24*(4), 365–84. https://doi.org/10.1007/s00787-015-0675-7

Vreeland, A., Gruhn, M. A., Watson, K. H. et al. (2019). Parenting in context: Associations of parental depression and socioeconomic factors with parenting behaviors. *Journal of Child and Family Studies*, *28*(4), 1124–33. https://doi.org/10.1007/s10826-019–01338–3

Wagner, K. D. (2003). Major depression in children and adolescents. *Psychiatric Annals*, *33*(4), 266–70. https://doi.org/10.3928/0048-5713-20030401-07

Wallace, D. (2011). Discriminatory mass de-housing and low-weight births: Scales of geography, time, and level. *Journal of Urban Health*, *88*(3), 454–68. https://doi.org/10.1007/s11524-011-9581-6

Wang, Y., & Dix, T. (2017). Mothers' depressive symptoms in infancy and children's adjustment in grade school: The role of children's sustained attention and executive function. *Developmental Psychology*, *53*(9), 1666–79. https://doi.org/10.1037/dev0000373

Waszczuk, M. A., Zimmerman, M., Ruggero, C. et al. (2017). What do clinicians treat: Diagnoses or symptoms? The incremental validity of a symptom-based, dimensional characterization of emotional disorders in predicting medication prescription patterns. *Comprehensive Psychiatry*, *79*, 80–88. https://doi.org/10.1016/j.comppsych.2017.04.004

Weems, C. F., Zakem, A. H., Costa, N. M., Cannon, M. F., & Watts, S. E. (2005). Physiological response and childhood anxiety: Association with symptoms of anxiety disorders and cognitive bias. *Journal of Clinical Child and Adolescent Psychology*, *34*(4), 712–23. https://doi.org/10.1207/s15374424jccp3404_13

Weersing, V. R., Jeffreys, M., Do, M. T., Schwartz, K. T. G., & Bolano, C. (2017). Evidence base update of psychosocial treatments for child and adolescent depression. *Journal of Clinical Child and Adolescent Psychology, 46*(1), 11–43. https://doi.org/10.1080/15374416.2016.1220310

Weinberg, M. K., Olson, K. L., Beeghly, M., & Tronick, E. Z. (2006). Making up is hard to do, especially for mothers with high levels of depressive symptoms and their infant sons. *Journal of Child Psychology and Psychiatry, 47*(7), 670–83. https://doi.org/10.1111/j.1469-7610.2005.01545.x

Weinberg, M. K., & Tronick, E. Z. (1996). Infant affective reactions to the resumption of maternal interaction after the still-face. *Child Development, 67* (3), 905–14.

Weinberg, M. K., Tronick, E. Z., Beeghly, M., Olson, K. L., Kernan, H., & Riley, J. M. (2001). Subsyndromal depressive symptoms and major depression in postpartum women. *American Journal of Orthopsychiatry, 71*(1), 87–97. https://doi.org/10.1037/0002-9432.71.1.87

Weiss, B., & Garber, J. (2003). Developmental differences in the phenomenology of depression. *Development and Psychopathology, 15*(2), 403–30. https://doi.org/10.1017/S0954579403000221

Weiss, B., Weisz, J. R., Politano, M., Carey, M., Nelson, W. M., & Finch, A. J. (1992). Relations among self-reported depressive symptoms in clinic-referred children versus adolescents. *Journal of Abnormal Psychology, 101*(3), 391–97. https://doi.org/10.1037/0021-843X.101.3.391

Werner-Seidler, A., Perry, Y., Calear, A. L., Newby, J. M., & Christensen, H. (2017). School-based depression and anxiety prevention programs for young people: A systematic review and meta- analysis. *Clinical Psychology Review, 51*, 30–47. https://doi.org/10.1016/j.cpr.2016.10.005

Wesselhoeft, R., Heiervang, E. R., Kragh-Sørensen, P., Juul Sørensen, M., & Bilenberg, N. (2016). Major depressive disorder and subthreshold depression in prepubertal children from the danish national birth cohort. *Comprehensive Psychiatry, 70*, 65–76. https://doi.org/10.1016/j.comppsych.2016.06.012

Wetter, E. K., & Hankin, B. L. (2009). Mediational pathways through which positive and negative emotionality contribute to anhedonic symptoms of depression: A prospective study of adolescents. *Journal of Abnormal Child Psychology, 37*(4), 507–20. https://doi.org/10.1007/s10802-009-9299-z

White, R., Pasco, M. C., Gonzales, N. A., Knight, G. P., & Burleson, E. (2019). US Mexican parents' use of harsh parenting in the context of neighborhood danger. *Journal of Family Psychology, 33*(1), 77–87. https://doi.org/10.1037/fam0000447

Wickramaratne, P., Gameroff, M. J., Pilowsky, D. J. et al. (2011). Children of depressed mothers 1 year after remission of maternal depression: Findings from the STAR*D-Child study. *American Journal of Psychiatry, 168*(6), 593–602. https://doi.org/10.1176/appi.ajp.2010.10010032

Williams, D. T. (2018). Parental depression and cooperative coparenting: A longitudinal and dyadic approach. *Family Relations, 67*(2), 253–69. https://doi.org/10.1111/fare.12308

Williamson, D. E., Birmaher, B., Axelson, D. A., Ryan, N. D., & Dahl, R. E. (2004). First episode of depression in children at low and high familial risk for depression. *Journal of the American Academy of Child and Adolescent Psychiatry, 43*(3), 291–97. https://doi.org/10.1097/00004583-200403000-00010

Wilson, S., & Durbin, C. E. (2010). Effects of paternal depression on fathers' parenting behaviors: A meta-analytic review. *Clinical Psychology Review, 30* (2), 167–80. https://doi.org/10.1016/j.cpr.2009.10.007

Wolff, J. C. & Ollendick, T. H. (2006). The comorbidity of conduct problems and depression in childhood and adolescence. *Clinical Child and Family Psychology Review, 9*(3–4), 201–20. https://doi.org/10.1007/s10567-006-0011-3

Wright, C. A., George, T. P., Burke, R., Gelfand, D. M., & Teti, D. M. (2000). Early maternal depression and children's adjustment to school. *Child Study Journal, 30*(3), 153–68.

Wu, Q., Feng, X., Hooper, E. G., Gerhardt, M., Ku, S., & Chan, M. H.-M. (2019). Mother's emotion coaching and preschooler's emotionality: Moderation by maternal parenting stress. *Journal of Applied Developmental Psychology, 65*, 101066. https://doi.org/10.1016/j.appdev.2019.101066

Yorbik, O., Birmaher, B., Axelson, D., Williamson, D. E., & Ryan, N. D. (2004). Clinical characteristics of depressive symptoms in children and adolescents with major depressive disorder. *The Journal of Clinical Psychiatry, 65*(12), 1654–59. https://doi.org/10.4088/JCP.v65n1210

Zeanah, C. H., Jr., & Zeanah, P. D. (2009). The scope of infant mental health. In C. H. Zeanah Jr. (Ed.), *Handbook of infant mental health* (3rd ed.). New York: Guilford Press, pp. 5–21.

Zhou, Q., Lengua, L. J., & Wang, Y. (2009). The relations of temperament reactivity and effortful control to children's adjustment problems in China and the United States. *Developmental Psychology, 45*(3), 724–39. https://doi.org/10.1037/a0013776

Zhou, Q., Main, A., & Wang, Y. (2010). The relations of temperamental effortful control and anger/frustration to Chinese children's academic achievement and social adjustment: A longitudinal study. *Journal of Educational Psychology, 102*(1), 180–96. https://doi.org/10.1037/a0015908

Cambridge Elements ☰

Child Development

Marc H. Bornstein

National Institute of Child Health and Human Development, Bethesda
Institute for Fiscal Studies, London
UNICEF, New York City

Marc H. Bornstein is an Affiliate of the Eunice Kennedy Shriver National Institute of Child Health and Human Development, an International Research Fellow at the Institute for Fiscal Studies (London), and UNICEF Senior Advisor for Research for ECD Parenting Programmes. Bornstein is President Emeritus of the Society for Research in Child Development, Editor Emeritus of Child Development, and founding Editor of Parenting: Science and Practice.

About the Series

Child development is a lively and engaging, yet serious and purposeful subject of academic study that encompasses myriad of theories, methods, substantive areas, and applied concerns. Cambridge Elements in Child Development proposes to address all these key areas, with unique, comprehensive, and state-of-the-art treatments, introducing readers to the primary currents of research and to original perspectives on, or contributions to, principal issues and domains in the field.

Cambridge Elements $^{\equiv}$

Child Development

Elements in the Series

.

Printed in the United States
by Baker & Taylor Publisher Services